SMILE A.   .N

Your recovery from burnout, breakdown and overwhelming stress

Anna Pinkerton

Smile Again

Your recovery from burnout,
breakdown and overwhelming stress

Copyright © Anna Pinkerton 2017
www. annapinkerton. com

ISBN-13: 978-1542794497

Powerhouse Publications
94/124 London Road,
Oxford
OX3 9FN

Print Edition

British Library Cataloguing in Publication Data.
A catalogue record for this book is available from
the British Library.

This book is dedicated to:

My two beautiful daughters Tess and Nell, and anyone buckling under the weight of stress

Reviews of Smile Again

'In the complexity and agony of burnout and breakdown Smile Again, is your companion to recovery. In this book Anna has achieved a comprehensive guide to recovering yourself from despair. Her use of simple images shows her deep understanding of the neuroscience of trauma but she manages to make it uncomplicated. If you are stressed, burnt out or feeling on the verge of breakdown this book can guide you to full health.

Having worked alongside Anna for several years now, I can see why she has become the "go to" expert for professionals and leaders who want to help themselves and their staff with the effects of stress. I highly recommend Anna's book Smile Again and indeed all her work.'

Emma Harrison CBE

'There are certain people you meet in your lifetime that are game changers. Anna is one of these. If you normally are the "strong" one but have been blindsided by an event which has left you struggling to function, then this book could save your life. Trauma by the way can come in many simple forms – a divorce, loss of your loved one, an accident, an attack. Anna talks honestly about the unspoken emotions we are taught to brush under the carpet and this book shows you that you aren't going mad, that life will get better and more importantly how to get back on track.'

Nicky Coffin, Management and Leadership Trainer and Performance Coach www.centredexcellence.co.uk

'Smile Again provides a down to earth view of the process of recovery from trauma. The programme provided through the book enables the traumatised person and their loved ones to begin the process of healing. Anna Pinkerton's approachable language and concepts engage the readers and make it possible for them to take a fresh look at a devastating subject, providing hope that it is possible to recover and then providing the practical means to begin that journey.

Though the book is aimed at those in the public eye, people who are not will find it easy to access. Anna Pinkerton presents information on the physiological and neurological aspects of trauma in an accessible way. Her ability to speak in everyday English and explain sometimes complicated concepts is exceptional and makes this book a resource that I can heartily recommend.'

Dr Lori Beth Bisbey, CPsychol, AFBPsS, CTS, DipFMSA, MEWI, WPCC, Consultant Psychologist, Whole Person Certified Coach, Author of Brief Therapy for Post-Traumatic Stress
www.bisbeyltd.com
www.wolfsfire.com

'Anna brings together her vast professional experience in the area of PTSD and marries it beautifully with her personal experience and wisdom. Her compassion, empathy as well as her extensive knowledge makes this a powerful book bringing solutions to a painful and difficult subject.

It's a book that's long overdue in a sector previously filled with beautiful personal accounts but which lack any real substance to help others, and academic tomes which offer brilliant advice but with little real depth of compassion or understanding.

Not only will this book help anyone who works with sufferers of PTSD but also be a shining star of hope for those who are in the grip of their own struggle.

This book truly shows you how to smile again.'

Lisa Turner, Author, Coach, Therapist, Trainer
www.psycademy.co.uk

'If you want a real smile, instead of a cover-up smile, read this book!'

Janet Jones, Author, Speaker, Photographer.
Founder of Happiness Millionaire Ltd

'Anna covers the topic of trauma with such sensitivity that you feel like she's seated right in front of you. She talks about the whys, what's and how's in a way that is easy to grasp and follow.'

Soila Sindiyo MSc. MPBsS.
Founder & Editor of The Divorce Magazine

'Smile Again is written with more than hope, it's written with the certainty that there is recovery after trauma. Anna Pinkerton re-classifies the breakdown after trauma as "traumatic breakdown" and this can only enhance our understanding of the complete brokenness that people feel. This way of thinking about this complete collapse is uplifting to individuals and organisations that have experienced a rupture to this degree.'

Tina Kothari, Entrepreneur, Author, Director
Another Way Associates

'As Anna leads you into the darkness of sudden trauma you can feel it in the pit of your stomach, and you can feel her love as she holds your hand and gently brings you back with simple ideas to rise up again.'

David Taylor, Coach, Speaker, Trainer,
Director of Insight The Freedom Factory

'Anna is a gifted therapist who has the ability to help people not just survive extra-ordinary trauma but to go on and thrive as a result of that experience. She is perceptive, wise and very, very funny. This practical, down to earth book provides real world strategies for anyone suffering from a traumatic experience. If you are suffering and Anna has shown up in your life, then she is, quite literally, your lifeline. Congratulations Anna for packaging your experience and wisdom into this book, it is truly a gift to the world.'

Bernadette Doyle, Entrepreneur
www.bernadettedoyle.com

Acknowledgements

The first thank you goes to my girls for being wonderful human beings, having to do without me far too much over the last few years and being my motivation when times have been tougher than we could've imagined. I'm so sorry for what you've been through, especially when I couldn't be the Mummy I wanted to be, you needed and deserved.

My next thank you is to all of my amazing and inspiring teachers from over the last 25 years. I have immense gratitude for Linda Chapman who has not only inspired me to be the best therapist I can be, but also the best version of me I can. I'm so grateful for the unending support and guidance I have received from Peter Orlandi-Fantini through tough and wonderful times alike. Huge thanks also to Anne Bramwell who has treated my physical injuries and for being so gentle and warm when I was so broken.

Thank you to Fiona Woodhead for her patience and talent in making professional images from my day-to-day sketches. Thank you to Stephanie J Hale for her gentle expertise in helping this book become a reality. Thank you to Ragina Johnson for her exquisite design.

I can't thank enough my incredible project manager and friend Nicola Morris for her support in the project of this book from beginning to the very end. On top of that, she has been by my side helping me believe when I couldn't. Thank you to my dear and cherished friend and colleague Jane Bytheway for being my soul-mate over 25 years and through the many 'swamps' of life we've encountered and still we laugh.

My dear thanks go also to Melina Abbott, Laura Atkinson, Dr Lori Bisbey, Bob Buckley, Bernadette Doyle, Heather Fowlie, Adele Jackson, Dr Louise Jordan, David Taylor.

A special thank you to my Mum and Dad who saw me injured. They rallied at speed with physical and financial help. My Mum has tirelessly thrown her support behind my recovery and my mission in helping broken people repair. Thanks and love to all my brothers: Neil for never failing to make me smile, and Sean for being on the end of Skype, and to Liam for staying in the country with hugs, dinners, and chats.

My last few years wouldn't have been complete or

possible without all my dear friends who I am truly blessed with. Enormous thanks for making me smile and belly laugh go to: Leeann Alameda, Caroline Channing, Belinda Heaney, Trish King, Judy Murray, Sharon Power, Debbie Richardson, the wonderful people where I live and all the Belfast Super Stars and My Tribe you know who you are!

Last but in no way least my eternal thanks to my clients and supervisees throughout the years who have been inspirational, and whose tremendous courage never fails to touch me, educate me and has consistently assisted me in digging deep.

With much love always, Anna x

Table of Contents

Preface

Bad stuff happens to good people all the time. Overwhelming stress happens to the very best of us. When the bad stuff is so bad, it takes you off your feet and shunts you sideways out of life as you knew it. The kind of 'bad' stuff I'm talking about here is where you are burning out, or breaking down. This is the stuff where you don't want to die, but you don't know how to live either. They say that 'what doesn't kill us makes us stronger,' but unfortunately, it feels like it breaks us first.

If you are left in this agonising stress too long, you can easily lose the desire and resources to live. Overwhelming stress causes a desolation of the mind, body, and soul which can cause burnout, breakdown, and what I call 'traumatic breakdown.' I call it this because in the very moment you know you can't take another thing, you may experience this rupture as a traumatic shock.

The seven processes that I talk about in this book are aimed at those of you who are traumatised to the point that you are struggling to function on an hour-to-hour, day-to-day basis.

If you suffer, or you know someone who continues to suffer for well over a month, I urge you now to reach out for help. It's really important you find someone who understands and is knowledgeable about what is happening to you because you are having a normal reaction to an extraordinary event or set of events. It is incredibly difficult to get through this alone whilst you feel so broken and whilst you cannot see your resources for yourself just now. I am not suggesting you need to be in therapy. I am suggesting that you simply take a step to reduce your suffering as quickly as possible. Your burnout and breakdown are upon you within seconds, but sadly the process of recovery is hundreds of thousands of times longer than that. It doesn't, however, have to be years and years of treatment either.

This storm of post-shock symptoms affects every single aspect of your life. No single part of your life remains unaltered. You are exhausted, anxious, and engulfed by it. You may have lost everything that you knew: every measurement that you knew to live life by has gone for a time. You've experienced the complete obliteration of all your previous coping skills, all your abilities and attributes that guided your days. The unknowing place that you are thrown into is overwhelmingly frightening and has you feeling that it's utterly insurmountable, certainly in the early hours and days.

Though it may seem insurmountable now, it absolutely is not. I set out to share my hope and my experiences of witnessing that people overcome the most atrocious experiences, including diagnosis of life-threatening illness, sexual assault, assault, domestic assault, life-saving surgery after injury, media assault, crashing depression. Over the years, I have consistently used simple images to help people understand overwhelming experiences. These will be dotted throughout the book to help you understand what's happening to you and your loved ones. I have developed this simple imagery to support explanation and explorations of what you might be going through when you cannot easily take in verbal communication alone due to changes in the brain. The use of the images reaches beyond the psycho-physiological impairment, offering you a real chance of feeling better fast and entering into recovery at a point in time when verbal therapy alone cannot fully assist you.

When trying to simplify such a complex subject, you run the risk of minimising it; I have endeavoured not to do that. This book is to help those of you who are suffering quietly from emotional and psychological injury and those of you for whom it is often impossible to reach out for support.

Bowing under the pressures of family life and work life is most people's dread and most people's humiliation. We're supposed to keep going, you see. There are few rewards for being the one who flags up stress as a life destroyer. How we treat people who burnout and breakdown is demonstrated to us every day in media and social media. We are 'shown' every day that prolonged stress causes us to burnout, yet still most stay smiling when inside they are in agony. The witnessing of this creates the perfect environment to breed thousands of people who will retreat and not reach out for help. The handling of this has to be on a cultural level and is where we have an opportunity to show and create a considerate environment for people who through prolonged stress have reached despair.

I'm on a mission to change what happens to people after they've experienced shocking and extraordinary events. We live in a world of looking at lost work hours and lost money. What about lost hours of happiness, or contentment, or joy? We just don't value this in the same way. Happiness and positivity lead to an upward spiral of happiness and positivity. If we valued this and helped people recover from tragedy, the work hours and money would take care of themselves.

I'd like to see us embrace and protect psychologically injured people; I know it's all been said before, but almost every day I hear of another person who is afraid to say how they truly feel for fear of judgement, of being ostracised. This is inexcusable in this day and age when we have so many resources at our fingertips to use for good.

I have spent nearly 25 years working with traumatised people and studying the subject of post-traumatic stress in one way or another. I draw on all of my research, my training and experience to be able to do the work I do today and to inform you in this book.

My development as a practitioner comes from so many varied disciplines and is informed by exceptional and learned masters in their field. I wanted this to be an easy-to-read informative book, so I have not dotted people's names throughout the book. At the end of the book, I include a list of the further reading, including the names of the people who have influenced me significantly through my life so far.

I want to be clear in this introduction that I have included the characteristics of recovery that I have encountered and observed. I include all of the processes, but they are just that – it is in no way a linear journey or prescription. Recovery from burnout and breakdown has an uncanny way of 'bouncing you' around in different directions. So for instance, although I believe in the process of recovery, I want to be clear that they are not steps – they are processes that must be engaged with and may have to be revisited more than once.

They are processes that need attention and need 'feeling' through. That does not mean lengthy, agonizing therapy, but it does mean you need to feel your way through a process of experience and understanding in order for you to move through it. I am saying you can't think yourself better – you cannot intellectualise your way through; it simply doesn't work that way.

So, when I talk about the characteristics of recovery as processes that's because I believe that to some extent you do need to be in it, experiencing and moving through it, rather than just viewing it. However, as long as you don't 'overthink' it, your intellect will be of great service to you on this journey.

The need to go backwards, forwards, up, down and round and round in our recovery process is not all bad. In the event of the brain and body needing to go back and revisit one of these processes to attend to something, you'll be glad to know the opposite also occurs. So, for instance you can make rapid gain, unexpected bits of recovery without very much attention to them whatsoever.

To be in the process of recovery means that you get the most control possible so you can navigate your recovery. What I mean is you are not thrown around like a ragdoll in a dog's mouth (although the early stages will feel much like that).

If you are struggling to manage any or all overwhelming symptoms, please know that the best way to look after yourself is to reach out for the help that is suitable for you. You are not alone, and recovery is an arm's length away.

When you feel you can't take another thing, or you feel you can't take anymore, I am writing this to you.

Introduction:
STRESS LOVES YOU NOT BEING FULLY HUMAN – So embrace all it is to be human and be yourself with a full range of feelings

Firstly, I know that you have enormous responsibilities for yourself, for others, for family, for friends, for work, for your future, and for their future, and you will be feeling dreadful that something has struck you down so dramatically. I want you to know now that it's truly okay and imperative that you take some time to get through this, to recover and heal. Burnout and breakdown don't happen in a minor way, and they require you to take major action in the short term to facilitate a thorough recovery. However hard it is to accept, you might find that you need to take two weeks off from work right away while you attend to what's happening to you. Two weeks now may well save you 20 weeks later. Having support whilst you work and recover simultaneously can reduce the pressure you experience and speed up recovery. Giving due time and consideration to yourself now reduces the likelihood of more suffering and prolonged recovery time. It's not forever; it's just for now.

The single most important thing to impart to you is that FEELINGS CAN'T BE WRONG. I bet you didn't know that! How you feel is never wrong. What you do with how you feel might not work for you, or might be difficult or even awful for others, but feelings are all OK. At the point of feeling you have no control over it. The feeling cannot be wrong, but what you do with the feeling, how you think about yourself, the world, others, and how you behave can work for or against you.

The other important thing to know really early is that you are experiencing what it's like when your brain goes into 'survival mode.' The early stages of burnout and breakdown are characterised by this onslaught.

Whilst everything in your life is rearranged after shocking events and/or burnout and breakdown, it is crucial to try at least to remember that you have overcome things before.

I understand that this is impossible for you certainly to begin with, to believe or remember. We are all a mixture of successes and failures; we have all got experience that will help us through this, but in the early hours and days and even weeks, it is impossible for us to remember or see this. I want you to try to remember or perhaps find someone to help you remember and know at least in a small way to begin with that you have overcome things before. You have risen to many challenges in your life, and you have supported others in their challenges too. Remembering this, even if you have to write it down on a post-it note, will help.

Remembering and being reminded of your resources and resilience is the most crucial aspect of your recovery. In the depths where despair takes you, we need help to remember our strengths we have used to overcome problems before. Consistent reminders of what's in your skills kit and not what's missing are very important. When you feel broken, it feels like nothing matters, but everything matters all at the same time. It takes a while for us to catch up with this, for our heads and hearts to connect again. Shocking events throw the brain into overdrive, so it's like living with the mainframe going into hyper-drive. You can feel totally under its brutal control at this point in the early stages; that's why being aware of what's in your skills kit already must be continually illuminated for you if not by you.

Keeping an eye on what's in your skills kit throughout episodes of despair and when you feel like you're going backwards gives a little nudge to the brain to start making new pathways. If, for instance, during a burnout and breakdown you have a well-played story or track record in your head such as 'I'm not strong,' 'I'm not good enough' that will be your belief. When you embark on recovery and healing, you get a chance to change the record and to make another start, another chapter of the story; in some instances, another record altogether.

However, when you feel broken and cannot repair quickly, you may feel at the mercy of this brutal fog, this trauma storm.

Keeping the Faith

When you're in the brutal storm of trauma, it simply is impossible to see the end of it, the endpoint. The desolation doesn't allow for an alternative – not at first. Glimpses of hope are the 'diamonds' for believing that you will come through it. These tiny glimpses in the trauma storm are the crystals lighting the path to recovery when you can't feel or see it. When the fog persists, the terror remains. When the fog recedes, hope is restored. Soul-deep wounding means you need a knowledgeable helper to help you believe that healing is possible. By soul, I mean the bit of you where your mind, body, physiology, and experience meet and make you be uniquely you.

Trauma storm disallows the possibility of hope; it throws you around, insisting that recovery is simply to be able to eat again, to simply be able to stop shaking again or to stop feeling nauseous. The trauma storm tends to foster negative hope, in that we lose the bad part of the trauma experience, and it almost never gives us a feeling that there will be any gains from this experience whatsoever.

If this book can give you more than hope, then I would say to you believe that this is the start of an amazing journey; you will have terrible times along the way, but the recovery is recovering all parts of you, of your soul. You get a chance to rediscover all parts of your soul. All that you were born with, born to be, want to be. It's a journey of discovery and rediscovery – though unfortunately, it happens to feel like being on a rollercoaster without a seatbelt. This amazing opportunity is shrouded in repeated episodes of devastation in the early stages. It doesn't stay that way. It gets easier and better.

What is overwhelming stress, burnout, and breakdown?

The above are all different ways of describing when one thing or many things have broken through your defences– where you have been shocked or incrementally exhausted by repetitive stress. I call it traumatic breakdown because of the experience of when one feels the resources go. You may well have a moment where you just cannot take any more. Can't get in the car to work, can't get in the train, and cannot face another demand.

No matter what character you are or what characteristics you have, every one of us has a propensity and vulnerability to experiencing burnout, breakdown, and stress. How come? Simply because we are alive; that's the only essential requirement. That does not mean that our vulnerabilities are not different (I talk about this later). It means that traumatic experiences are by their very nature indiscriminate and able to take anyone 'down'. I might repeat myself a fair bit with this reality, but if it hasn't taken you off your feet, 'taken you down' 'overwhelmed all your senses' then it is not burnout, breakdown, overwhelming or traumatic breakdown. Every single person has a limit to the psychological and emotional strain they can take. There are no exceptions to this.

Breakdown or burnout is as close as one will get to describing the complete and utter rupture people experience. Not one person I have worked with in over 20 years has come to tell me they have been traumatised. They nearly always will describe themselves as anxious, terrified, broken, hopeless, depressed, but never traumatised. So, this book is about sharing the characteristics of the recovery journey I have found in helping 'broken' people repair.

The accommodation of burnout in our culture has basically been accepted. We are prepared to push somebody beyond their limit and allow the body and mind to breakdown. The early warning signs, of which there will be many, are ignored, and someone with tenacity is rewarded in the short term. In the longterm, extending one's emotional and psychological health consistently will eventually be taken care of by the body and mind by burning out or breaking down. Some attention to our societal and cultural acceptance of self-destruction above self-care is part of looking after the emotionally and psychologically injured. Perhaps this book, its exploration, and discussion of supporting vulnerable people, will shine some light on this.

To support the ease of reading this book, I am going to continue calling the experience of overwhelming stress 'burnout' and 'breakdown'. This label is for ease of understanding the complete and utter overwhelming of a person's functioning, and acknowledging that the breakdown itself can be experienced as a traumatic event.

Burnout and breakdown are:

There are two avenues to burnout and breakdown and becoming traumatised. They are the Type 1 and Type 2.

Type 1 is a sudden event with no anticipation whatsoever. That might be an assault, an accident, an earthquake, something where you have no knowledge of it coming along at all.

Type 2 is a slow 'drip-drip' effect of an accumulation of stresses. An incremental and consistent pressure like work-related stress, bullying, abuse. Eventually, the brain just can't deal with it, and it might lead to depression or anxiety or a traumatic breakdown.

Do both types require the same kind of recovery process?

In some ways they do. There are specific things you can do with Type 1. If you've had Type 1 only, and you've had a one-off event, they tend to be easier to treat and quicker to recover from. But of course, sometimes people can have a slow build-up of stressors but also have a shocking event happen as well. So every single individual has a unique past impacting the complexion of their burnout or breakdown.

My belief in feeling better fast is, first of all, giving you the information you need about what's happening. Everybody goes through the same processes. You might go through it more slowly or more quickly, but also, every single element of it is different for everybody. I do think the process is similar , though. It's worth mentioning here that because burnout and breakdown 'scrambles' the mind for a while, because of the sheer neurological overload, the stages will bounce around in an extraordinary fashion for most people.

Once you've been traumatised, is it possible to suffer another trauma?

Yes, it is possible; indeed, you are much more vulnerable to further traumatisation once you have been traumatised, particularly if you have not fully recovered. This is a major reason for seeking proper guidance through burnout and breakdown. Firstly, to feel better quickly, and secondly, so that it doesn't persist in making you consistently vulnerable in the future. That's why I believe in support that provides a thorough, robust recovery, so it lasts a lifetime.

The seven processes to feeling better fast become part of your skillskit for life. For instance, one of the things you need to do in the beginning is find inner safety. It doesn't matter from which path they've come to it – once a person has experienced being able to find themselves safety, and even conjure up images of safety, this will never be forgotten and will go with them in their 'skillskit for life.'

Often, a lot of the symptoms that come as a consequence of the traumatic breakdown are because the BRAIN DOESN'T KNOW THAT THE TRAUMA IS OVER, so the brain keeps telling the mind and body that it's still in danger. The brain is 'over-stimulated' and responds as though it's continually under threat. This means reducing stimuli and understanding 'overreactions' to stimuli. As the brain recovers, the responses calm too.

Other stresses and further adversity, of course, can also be experienced as actual traumatic events. Further stresses known as secondary stressors are separate experiences away from the initial incident(s), but it is necessary to be mindful how a person who is already traumatised experiences them. The traumatised person's mechanisms for moderating reactions and formulations of safety are already out of action, partly by 'injured psychobiology,' and partly by the initial event. A frightening but not endangering event can, therefore, be perceived as life-threatening. It's really important to be mindful of the things you choose to do early in recovery, and the kinds of things the people caring for you can do to help also.

Slow-to-build-up burnout and breakdown

Before we go on to look at the specific characteristics of healthy recovery, it is useful to spend some time acknowledging the complexity of slow-to-build-up burnout and breakdown.

Slow-to-build-up burnout and breakdown can be an incredibly cruel conclusion to someone's attempts at surviving multiple stresses. As I was saying before, each pattern of burnout and breakdown is as unique as a fingerprint. I guess the important thing here is to make the distinction for you between two types of breakdown. Slow-to-build-up breakdowns can be characterised two ways, I believe. Firstly, it is where there is a long history of mainly different types of manageable stressors. This may take the form of bereavement, redundancy, financial problems and then something that forces through your resources once and for all, causing a rupture in your coping mechanisms and overwhelming you, prompting a collapse.

You might find it's hard to pinpoint one thing that you feel justifies the magnitude of your breakdown. For you, it can be terribly upsetting and un-dignifying to feel as though you have no real reason or no 'acceptable' reason to warrant the complete and utter desolation you are now experiencing. For you, it is crucial that you are helped to understand that you have not knowingly brought this upon yourself.

Secondly, the other avenue in slow-to-build-up breakdown can be where someone has been emotionally and psychologically injured within childhood. This basically means that they have for many years been functioning with a skills kit that was never allowed to be fully equipped. Early emotional and psychological injuries can affect a person's ability to develop into the people they truly were born to be and want to be, and to have the lives they dream of. It can even affect that person's ability to dream and have vision at all. We are all at the mercy of our early templates (our early experiences). People with trauma templates (difficult early life experiences) are at the mercy of something that has the ability to cause debilitation many years after childhood. In my experience, adulthood traumas, for example Type 1 unanticipated traumas, can reignite early childhood trauma templates. With support, this can be seen as an opportunity for the person to develop themselves in the direction that they desire in order to be free of something that might be privately shackling them, and for them to release their creativity and new dreams. Slow-to-build-up burnout and breakdown can take longer to recover from; that can simply be because of the length of time we have adapted to much earlier experience, and it may take a little while for us to find our pathway through to recovery.

Characteristics of slow-to-build-up burnout and breakdown tend to be the astonishing ability to live with and not to pay attention to emotional pain. For these people in recovery, it is important to illuminate that no emotion lasts forever. If emotions are permitted – in other words felt and moved through – they simply go through us or wash over us; they do not last. It's only when we cleverly label a feeling with judgements and attach meaning to feelings that they last and become 'sticky'. On an energetic level, this can mean that we have an internal juggling of emotion that we are trying to avoid. We have made by accident or design our own internal emotional 'minefield.' What a precarious and dangerous place for us to reside! And, as previously stated, if we reside in such a difficult emotional place we suffer energetically, i.e. we cannot focus on the things that are good for us, and we learn to 'click off' to the intolerable turmoil and numb it.

All of the processes I include in this book apply to all people in burnout and breakdown no matter what avenue they were thrown into it from.

Smile Again is about those events that you don't see coming that devastate you. It's also about sharing my view about how you might best work through such devastating events. I believe that you can recover, heal, and move through to a better and stronger self. I believe you can go on to find wonderful opportunities for yourself and things to offer the world as well as contentment and happiness.

This book is about recovering from devastating life events. It's born out of thousands of hours of experience and how I have come to find characteristics of all recovery. It's very important to point out that this is based upon my experience with victims of trauma, people affected by gunshot wounding, knife wounding, assault, rape, sexual assault, media attack, surgical mistakes, workplace bullying, earthquake, domestic assault, childhood trauma, chronic overwork. No one way fits all. The reason to write this is in the hope that people may recognise themselves or others within it and suffering is reduced.

I am absolutely passionate about being part of a culture and society that supports people to recover, heal, and move through things when their hearts feel broken, their lives ripped to shreds, and they can see nothing but darkness and agony.

I want to provide nuggets of hope when people have none. Nuggets of knowledge when they feel they can't take any more.

No matter how much inner turmoil you're in, you are programmed not to stop. When you are shunted into burnout and breakdown, you are forced in the most brutal fashion into stopping. This is incredibly frightening, especially to those of you who are used to striving and being there to support others.

For those who have had a 'slow onset' build up to the traumatic breakdown, you may well be those same people who struggle to stop, take care of yourself and reach out for help. If the book helps you know that finding support even for the simplest of things starts your road to full recovery, then great.

I want there to be a move towards people reaching for help when they need it, without shame; to gain knowledge and support when they are ready for it. The consequence of year upon year of inner turmoil is hundreds of thousands of work hours lost; happy hours lost, lives lost, and opportunities lost. It doesn't have to be that way.

The personal and societal cost is literally a secret 'inner turmoil' that pervades our communities, at home and work. Suppressed stress leads to depression and many other mental health issues.

These include:

- Addiction: excessively turning to alcohol, food, drugs, gambling, buying, in an attempt to tolerate and ignore the inner turmoil.

- Cutting off (dissociating) from intense feelings to avoid being further overwhelmed, and then living below the full range of feelings and personal potential.

- Poor self-esteem and self-worth reducing your ability to be out in the world fully. In the extreme, you can feel worthless and swing from feeling good or really bad, leading to consistent...

- Suicidal thoughts, actual self-harm and suicide attempts. This is what lack of full emotion and feelings of worthlessness can often lead to:

- Chronic problems in connecting with others.

- Difficulty having or maintaining intimate relationships.

- Long-term anxiety and depression without realising the core cause. This then compounds feelings of worthlessness and inadequacy, and so the cycle continues.

Without a larger, more embracing response to the emotionally and psychologically injured, we basically help to produce hundreds of thousands of people suffering from depression. Obviously people suppress their distress for many different reasons, but if we were to live in an atmosphere of support and provided it without judgement, we would make great strides in reducing the mental health epidemic we are seeing. We simply have not decided to make it this way.

I am passionate about changing this, and I am privileged to see people pick up their lives with renewed purpose and fervour when they didn't feel that it was possible.

Burnout and breakdown when you're in the public eye

Bad stuff happens to good people in the public eye all the time too. When bad stuff happens to you, it's witnessed, it's scrutinized and often becomes part of a collapse that's totally preventable. When shocking events happen to those who usually inspire, serve, support, and employ others, the public element is excruciating. You are not in an environment where the psychologically and emotionally injured are considered compassionately. People in public life are acutely aware of this. It is demonstrated to you every day in the media and social media. The brutality with which people in public life are treated is confirmed to you every day. Therefore, the level of fear you face in burnout and breakdown is compounded by the extraordinary scrutiny you are subjected to. As you know, your most vulnerable experiences are followed and watched; interpreted and misinterpreted by people behind cameras, people with notepads, recordings, community gossip, admirers and denouncers. We are all responsible for this painful place you are put in and onlookers are just mostly glad it is not happening to them. It does not have to be this way.

In public life but private turmoil

The complexity and far-reaching effects of having your physical and mental health under scrutiny are something the everyday person could not possibly imagine. Not only do you run the risk of having your health become public knowledge, you also, sadly, run the risk of this actually causing you further injury. For example, the actress who is feeling at the edge of her mental health becomes hounded by the press with cameras pointing at her and reporters 'door-stepping' her, actually worsening her mental state. This isn't reporting alone; this actually causes further emotional and psychological injury. People in the public eye know this all too well, which often entraps them to suffer in silence for way longer than is necessary or helpful. The reality of entrapment in a situation is discussed later, but if someone cannot mobilise to help themselves because there are people hounding them, the situation is totally out of their control, and it can become an intolerable experience. Those who are not left in privacy to receive help are further hurt. This is on two levels: firstly because there is a sense of public humiliation, and secondly because physiologically they are being triggered into further distress, causing increased stress chemicals and fears for their safety. This is no joke; it's real.

I know that many people will say that if you work in public life, then you invite this. I entirely disagree. Someone who chooses to work in public life and serve others, be it through whatever avenue, should not have to tolerate abusive and dangerous behaviour towards them. People have often decided to serve the community by entertaining us, for instance; does this truly permit us to abuse their mental health?

People who live and work in public life risk public demise when they are faced with burnout or breakdown. This is a perfect example of what people DO NOT need when they have been traumatised by an emotional collapse whatever the reason. If someone in the public eye has broken down or is close to breaking down, they need understanding, time, and support to find their route to recovery.

One of the things that prompted me to write this book was having worked with people in public life who are stripped of everything they've worked for including their livelihood and that of their family. The brutality and mass voyeurism at the 'fall' of successful people sickens me. There is no need for us to behave in this way towards another's turmoil. Look at the treatment of Tulisa Contostavlos and Beth Tweddle; what do we gain from the vicious destruction of another's character? What must be understood is that this can affect people for a lifetime. It can affect someone's health, both emotionally and physically. No one has the right to cause damage to another person. If we accept this way of being now, we also have the power to open our hearts and do the exact opposite. For instance, we can decide not to buy into it, literally and philosophically. We can decide not to share it, and so not perpetuate it. We all have that power.

The daily portrayal of someone's burnout and breakdown within the media and now social media persists to prolong the agony of people who live and work in public life. To my mind, everyone deserves to be able to recover from burnout and breakdown and deserves the right to access support before breakdown if at all possible. The courage public figures find to support their reputation and to support their public role, whether they be lawyers, doctors, actors, sports stars, or entertainers, is incredible. Our collective delight in seeing someone collapse is, as you might have gathered, something I feel very strongly about, and it's time (long overdue) to commit to ending this.

The lack of privacy makes it almost impossible for public figures to access ordinary services. This can be due to fear of exposure of their vulnerability, difficulty asking for help, and a lack of discretion in public services.

This lack of opportunity to get support leads to further isolation. For people who work and live in public life, it is difficult for them to heal. You are used to being at the 'top of your game,' and you have worked hard to be there. You often have hundreds if not thousands of staff you feel responsible for, and fans who you've never met but you feel some responsibility for and who are watching from the 'wings.'

To be shunted from your place in the world is literally unbearable. Not only do you have to recover from the tragedy you have experienced, but you also miss out on the life that you have built and striven for. The fall can be painful and long. Being shunted from your high-level performance comes with a fear that it will never come back. This can often mean sporting chances are missed; hundreds of thousands of pounds are lost in real terms as well as lost opportunities. It's not a case of simply losing what you knew, and also losing livelihood and income; it is also the case that you can see no future at all. Often, someone will lose their public reputation through no fault of their own; this has devastating effects on their ability to recover.

Those living and working in inner turmoil can be terrified that others will find out; again, this compounds the feelings of shame. High profile, affluent people frequently feel that they must be able to recover by themselves. They can also feel that their 'privileged' position and wealth means they should not outwardly suffer and that they are on some level ashamed that their wealth has not protected them from this. Many people have said to me, 'I have no right to complain; I have all this luxury and privilege,' and my retort is, 'That's how indiscriminate trauma is; nothing can protect you from it.' An early preoccupation with entrepreneurial men and women is a fear that their reputation and future success will be sullied by their new vulnerability. Others will be concerned that others will 'prosper while they stagnate.' This may well be true for a time, but when you start to attend to the inner pains and transform the agony through working towards recovery you'll actually find that you will be more successful and live with more ease in every area of your life.

BLAME: SHAME & JUDGEMENT – STRESS loves this combination and will help create burnout and breakdown

My thinking is that the quickest and most effective beginning to any recovery journey is to wrestle feelings of blame, shame, and judgement.

Let's start with blame. It is incredibly difficult in a culture that blames and shames you for being human, not to blame yourself. Blame serves to distance people from the reality of their own vulnerabilities and distances us from the fact that bad stuff is simply indiscriminate. How scary is it for us all to be vulnerable to traumatic experience, vulnerable to stress, vulnerable to accident, vulnerable to natural disasters? Of course we want to distance ourselves from this reality. All that's required to have bad things happen to you is to be alive. That is the only requirement, and therefore, we are all possible victims. Trouble is our fears often paralyse us and can end up making us more susceptible. Our 'carry on regardless' culture can lead to lack of robustness when stresses pitch up in life. People in general – not all but most – are incredibly uncomfortable being around someone who is burning out or in breakdown. There are several reasons for this. Firstly, there is a very real physiological experience we have whilst being close to the agony of someone else's symptoms of dysregulation (the medical term for the symptoms where someone cannot calm themselves, who have heightened emotions as well as anxiety, heart racing, sweating, etc.) Secondly, people can feel that they will become somehow 'contaminated' by that person's distress. Certainly (likely subconsciously) people can become anxious about their own mental health vulnerabilities. As previously stated, if we were living in an atmosphere of solidarity and support, when overwhelmed with stress we would all be giving energy to an atmosphere where if somebody becomes emotionally and psychologically injured, everyone gets feedback that, however difficult, it will never be utterly catastrophic. Whilst our discomfort in being around somebody else's distress persists, we only persist in feeding back to ourselves the bare isolation we can be in. So, actually the bigger picture is to try to overcome one's discomfort and reach out to others to help allay distress, disarray, and isolation. I talk about this later when looking at how one might support someone after burning out or breaking down.

In the short term, the culture of blame serves this all very well because whilst we blame the victim for being overwhelmed and its devastating result, we go some way to distancing ourselves from the possibility of that type of event happening to us. If you can blame the individual or group of individuals for what is happening to them, then you protect yourself from the very real possibility that one day it could be you. The resultant effect of blaming the person or people even on a subconscious level transfers to people in this fragile state. This enhances their feelings of blame for themselves and their loneliness. In other words, the usual reaction to this pervasive culture of blame is to turn it upon the self. The person blaming themselves for what happened to them consequently feels the need to isolate themselves further; this then permits people to stay away from the terror they may feel whilst someone experiences this emotional overwhelming and turmoil, and so the cycle continues.

Isolation of people in emotional agony is dangerous. Fruitless blame turns into shame, and people want to hide all the more, relinquishing us all from the responsibility of care. Hiding oneself and being left in agony leads to hopelessness. Those people who 'roll their sleeves up' and overcome their own fears and persist with being with the person in turmoil are helping that person on many levels deal with the despair.

It is pivotal to your recovery that you find people that believe you will recover. It is also incredibly powerful for you to hear from others who have been through burnout and breakdown and come through it. You may construe people's distance as if you are being blamed for your own frailty. I feel this is rarely the case, but more likely they don't know how to help.

The blame myth

A cultural atmosphere of blaming people who fall victim to burnout and breakdown leads to shame. So let's look at how we can help explain what burnout and breakdown is and why there is no shame in it.

The type of event that precipitates traumatic burnout and breakdown is completely out of your control. If it is within your control, it rarely is traumatic. That does not mean to say that there were not indicators of severe and chronic stresses. If you did not know you'd collapse, then you cannot be to blame.

Anyone can be a victim of an unexpected, freakish event; it is entirely indiscriminate.

If it could happen to anyone, and it's an event or set of events that are completely out of your control, then it is impossible for you to be to blame for it. If someone could save themselves from a traumatic experience, they would, but of course they cannot. The flipside of that is: if they knew the traumatic event was coming, it wouldn't be traumatic or overwhelming in the same way because they would have the time to become prepared for it. Burnout and breakdown only happen when every resource, resilience, and defence you have is overwhelmed by something bigger than all of your strengths put together. Sometimes people will describe this as 'something bigger than me happened.'

My belief is that this is about reducing suffering fast and effectively and also preserving energy that blame and shame take away from your recovery. If you are spending time in blame when you simply cannot be to blame (which then 'mutates' to shame), you are expending energy that can be used to heal.

It's essential you look at our pervasive culture of shaming and blaming. My belief is people suffer unnecessarily longer because of the culture of blame and shame that we live within. We all have the opportunity to reflect on our attitudes and our discomforts around emotionally and psychologically injured people. You too can be part of a culture of warmth and consideration if you decide to be. Keeping a distance as a protective mechanism against difficult and uncomfortable realities like trauma will not protect us from it; in fact, I would go so far as to say it does the exact opposite.

Shame

Blaming oneself or feeling blamed leads to shame. Shame can be felt on a continuum. In its weakest form, it is a feeling of the pinch of embarrassment of the self for someone's thoughts or actions; at the strongest end of the continuum, it is overwhelming shame, which is paralysing.

When you are paralysed physically or emotionally after devastating events, you will find it takes considerable effort to get on to a path of recovery. All entrapment makes things feel worse. The feeling of not being able to do anything towards your recovery can be utterly terrifying and then in time demoralising. This, in turn, causes the body to respond with fear and anxiety, and then further increased adrenalin and cortisol and other stress hormones. There are significant biochemical changes during a chronic and sudden stress. Long-term stress can cause interruptions to learning, interruptions to the normal trajectory of development, to your choices and your ability to perceive differences between threatening and non-threatening stimuli. An example of this is war veterans who have developed unpredictable and aggressive outbursts at loud noises or unexpected movements by others because they perceive it as a threat to life, like being on hyper-alert all of the time. Whilst there is an increase in stress hormones that cause the body to be in alert mode, there is a reduction in the hormones such as serotonin and oxytocin endorphins which provide a physiological environment of calm. Low levels of serotonin cause anger, irritability, low mood, and depressions. When you feel you can't 'pull' yourself out of this, you may feel ashamed that you cannot cure yourself, that you cannot 'pull yourself together.' This may once again lead to embarrassment and shame, then paralysis and inertia, and so the cycle continues.

You can help yourself immediately by dropping the blame and the shame, and by deciding to treat yourself with kindliness and companionship for what you've been through.

Judgement

Suspend all judgement of yourself and replace it with NOTICING.

If we were all committed to doing this, we would

all lose so many fewer hours of happiness. It takes so much less energy to notice things and notice feelings than it does to see them, feel them, and then overlay them with judging. This goes for judging ourselves and judging others. By judging, I mean when you are able to know how you're feeling but you tell yourself 'Get yourself together you pathetic moron. I run a multi-million-pound company – now look at me!' Judgement hurts you and keeps you still and in suffering. Though it's incredibly common, it doesn't help your recovery, but it takes a little time to adapt to thinking otherwise and to practice 'NOTICING.'

The more positive energy you can hold on to, the greater chance you give yourself to be on an upward spiral of recovery rather than a downward spiral of pain. The upward spiral of recovery is the desired shape towards your healing. Upward spiral means that the weight of your experience is underneath you, and you stand on top of it, like at the top of the mountain looking down.

When you are on an upward spiral of recovery, you are making steps towards being on the top of your experience. As you move up the spiral of recovery, you are more and more able to tap into all of the resources that you already have and to learn new ones. The brutality of burnout and breakdown is made all the worse when you feel you cannot help yourself, and you cannot see a way out. The upward spiral, however slow it might feel, allows you glimpses of tools that you can use to aid your recovery journey; things like being able to take a walk or having a chat with friends. These simple things allow at some level your mind body and soul to know that recovery is possible. When you are in an upward spiral, your ability to tap into and create endorphin release and other naturally occurring 'mood boosters' increases, and so, the upward spiral continues. As you gain feedback, you naturally become more positive about your ability and chance to recover.

The downward spiral, of course, is the exact opposite of that. This means it feels increasingly difficult to get on top of and master your experience. As you feel yourself slipping down the spiral, the weight of your experience is felt more and more heavily. So, when you are not at the top of it learning from it and mastering it, you increasingly feel the weight of it. This logically leads to an increasing sense of despair, hopelessness, and often depression. Whilst you become overwhelmed by these feelings, your ability to find it within yourself to reach out for support and to involve yourself in activities becomes increasingly remote. It's absolutely vital for you to know that this is a normal feature of a recovery process; as I said before, it isn't in most cases a straightforward journey; it's not an A-Z roadmap of recovery. It's much more like an 'A-R-Z-M-B-A-D-Z roadmap to recovery.'

The recovery process is often an unpleasant 'dance' between being in an upward spiral and being in a downward spiral from day-to-day or even hour-to-hour.

Recovery and healing become more and more apparent once you're in the downward spiral less and less. The upward spiral begins to contain all of your old learning that has been available to you and all of your new learning too. It's so important to remember that all of your learning is never forgotten; it will be part of your experience and your skills kit for life.

Figure 1. Image of downward spiral

Image 1 showing the spiral downwards, where experience gets the better of you and becomes a weight that is on top of you, rather than you

being on top of your experience. Every burnout and breakdown start like this.

Fearing the unknown

It's really important that I tell you now that everybody fears the unknown. Whilst burnout and breakdown take you away from everything that you knew, loved and didn't love, it's put you in a place of not knowing anything at all. This, I promise you, doesn't last, but it does cause you great pain and fear. It's expected that you'd be afraid whilst you cannot see a way out of this turmoil, whilst you can't see a way back to the life you had or a way forward to a new one. It's helpful to find people, writing, songs or anything that helps you manage the fear you're in and helps you believe this won't last; because it won't. Nothing lasts forever, including an unknowing place.

I have sat with dozens of people who struggle to keep faith that better is to come. This can be even when they have made gigantic strides within their own trauma recovery story. You may find this too. Even when the trauma storm is passing, panic of not fully recovering can cruelly catch you unawares again. This stage of the process is so difficult because you have absolutely no idea what the future holds. If all markers of life are gone, all vision is gone; all dreams are gone in an instant too. How scary to suddenly find your landscape devoid of all the things familiar, and all the people, and feelings that are familiar too. We're hardwired to imagine the future, to visualise it and work towards it. The cruel reality when you're in burnout and breakdown is that you lose your vision in the short term; you lose your future, but you have a terrifying present also. What is hard to bear is whilst you wrestle this unknown and whilst you navigate yourself through your recovery, your future is not lost. Your future is continually forming in the background whilst you recover; you simply cannot see it from behind the fog at this point. Which is why I'm saying this to you now early on for you to believe at some level that your future is formulating in the background. Whilst you recover and heal, your subconscious is noting its increased skills kit, your small gains, your large gains, and your dreams. Your whole system, mind, body, and soul is getting feedback all the time every day that you survive, and every ounce of healing is being noted. When your 'trauma storm' is at its most brutal, your feedback (however basic) is that you survive that day when you least believe you can. It's like your subconscious – your soul is cogitating and formulating your vision as you get on with the healing project of everyday. Very few of us are keen to be in an unknowing place, but this won't persist; you will make gains and certainties along the way. You will find you become increasingly aware of your knowledge, skills, and your likes and dislikes; your comfort, your anxieties hour-to-hour and day-to-day. This becomes your foundation, however rudimentary at first. A place where you can grow and be within the life you desire and within the life that you strive for.

Speedy and lifelong recovery should be open to everyone.

For people who live in the public eye, adversity has an added element of scrutiny, humiliation, and shame. It is this that leads to despair and which prolongs suffering and prevents people getting the help they need.

Looking for the right help that suits you can be difficult when you are so vulnerable. Sometimes it is simply because you have lost the confidence to even pick up the phone or go to see your GP. It is this small, simple, but very important step that makes your recovery start. It is useful to remind people that if you are reaching out for professional help, perhaps you initially speak to your GP, and certainly find someone who has experience in post-traumatic work. I have added a list of resources that I have respect for at the back of this book.

Is full recovery possible?

'Yes, full recovery is possible'! I would never have set out on this project if I didn't believe that and know it. It might change you, but recovery and healing are achievable.

If you reach out to work with somebody to recover, it's imperative that they believe that full recovery is possible. I'm not going to sit on the fence about this one! If you're sat with someone who doesn't believe recovery is possible or who is not willing to say they believe in recovery, the chances are you won't be able to recover with their support. If the person guiding you through this arduous process doesn't believe in recovery, it is likely that subconsciously that belief will ensure that you don't. That is not to say that a practitioner would want this for you, but soul-centred belief is imperative. Conversely, the believing practitioner cannot prescribe the exact process or timing of your recovery either.

I want to share that the fastest, most effective and thorough recovery is what we are working towards. Of course, there is always the possibility and reality that your journey is hindered or is ruptured by other things happening, but the aim is to smooth your recovery journey as best as possible. Unexpected difficulties are always a possibility for people. Belief and vision regarding recovery, however, are a necessary core belief with the awareness that one must be adequately prepared for other 'curveballs' being thrown.

For someone who is injured at the soul-deep level, it is crucial that they hear and experience people around them believing they will come through this. This is something that close family and close friends can help with. The initial episodes of despair can be helped by being near a person who believes you can come through this, or in actual fact, somebody who has been through it and come through it even more so.

Recovery is all about working towards a thorough understanding of our own unique breakdown. Every burnout and breakdown has a unique pattern to it. There are common features with everyone, but each pattern of burnout and breakdown is as unique as fingerprints. Full and lifelong recovery is about discovering the features that make the pattern and is about discovering each bit that hurts and needs healing.

My idea of recovery is twofold: firstly, that you get to the point of recovery, meaning you know the terrible thing has happened, but it's just a memory. Secondly, that your recovery is so thorough that the tragedy is over, and there is no need for the brain and body to keep reacting and causing stress related to it.

What's covered in the rest of the book?

The book covers the definitions of traumatic and shocking events as these are almost always features of burnout and breakdown. We'll look at the two different ways of getting to burnout and breakdown.

There are two ways burnout and breakdown can become traumatic: either it's a one-off event, where something so shockingly horrific happens, and there's no anticipation of it; it shunts you out of your life and everything that you knew. Then there's also a burnout and breakdown that is precipitated by multiple events, multiple stresses that build up, maybe over months and even years, and then suddenly, it gets to breaking point. The build-up is gradual, but the moment of overwhelming is felt like a sudden, shocking event in itself. Everyone has a limit, and we often don't know that that's the case or what that limit is until we hit it. The mind and the body can only cope with so much before it requires us to take note. Unfortunately, sometimes this grinds us to a halt.

So, we'll look at:

1. Sudden shocking breakdowns

2. Slow-to-build breakdowns

3. The seven processes that I believe are relevant in helping to give some structure to a complex route to feeling totally recovered from trauma.

The book is structured by being clear about the indisputable necessary elements that play a crucial part in healthy, thorough recovery. Parts of the book are necessarily repetitive in the acknowledgement that this will more than likely be the kind of book that people dip into a bit at a time. The book goes on to be structured around the seven processes to feeling better fast. These processes are characteristics of recovery that I believe in, each one being interrelated and supportive of the other. For instance, in the list below, you can see that knowledge and safety are close together. Knowledge about what is happening to you when you are terrified and desolate can begin to sow the seeds of feeling safe again. If you do not understand why your symptoms are there, or that they are a normal reaction to an abnormal event or set of events, you are unlikely to make any gain in feeling safe. Similarly when you can see glimpses of vision and excitement about your future once again, a little bit more **healing** can happen, and more **knowledge** about yourself is gained.

The 7 processes towards recovery and healing (numbered at the beginning of appropriate chapter):

1. KNOWLEDGE – STRESS is CRAZY, you are NOT – gain knowledge about what's happening

2. SAFETY – STRESS hates safety – slow down and find your 'soft place to fall'

3. CARE ABOUT YOU – STRESS THRIVES ON YOU HATING YOURSELF – beat it with love and kindness

4. HELP – your antidote to stress – allow help from professionals, friends, and family

5. REFLECT & ATTEND – meet and treat yourself with kindness, STRESS HATES that

6. HEALING – smoothing out your STRESS marks

7. VISION & MOVING ON – integrating your skillskit and dealing with STRESS once and for all

How will it help you?

Virtually no one feels better if they don't understand what's happening to them. One of the critical features about burnout, breakdown, and chronic stress is that it is so completely devastating to all your senses and inner strengths it feels utterly impossible to believe you will recover. It is incomprehensible that you can feel so broken and be fixed; you may have never experienced such 'overwhelm' or have ever seen anyone experience anything like this before. Every component of this journey is easier if you have the information about it and then the information to help you to recover and heal.

I intend to share with you that there's hope first of all, and there is certainty when you can grasp it. I'm sharing that it is absolutely likely that you'll be able to recover, and you can recover to the point where you actually feel better than ever and stronger than ever before. The body and mind are very good at battling on, and you can re-learn how to look after yourself in the way that aids recovery not hinders it. Countless thousands of us are taught to swallow our true feelings and 'grin and bear it.' We all have a unique pattern of emotional behaviour that is formed early in life and gets further endorsed into adulthood. This naturally leads us to develop a unique personal pattern of emotional acceptability. This pattern of emotional acceptability is very relevant in recovery after burnout and breakdown. Some of it is helpful in recovery, and some of it isn't.

I talk about this later as the emotional modus operandi (E.M.O.). There is also a silent acceptability about what is tolerable in our families, communities, and our society. Sometimes you'll be lucky enough to navigate yourself around these, and other times you won't.

It's a covert emotional operation which you will become increasingly aware of.

Where do you start with such a vast subject?

The book is going to start by looking at the kind of recovery that is robust and lasting, and how shame can hinder our recovery. It will then go on to look at the seven processes which are characteristic of all recovery journeys. For victims and those looking after them, it is important to me to set out what somebody might be suffering from. Information is crucial to reducing anxiety and the fear of the unknown. I want you to be able to find quickly the different kinds of symptoms you can have in burnout and breakdown so that you can see and understand them speedily and get on the journey to recovery.

Are all burnouts, breakdown, stress reactions the same?

Do a war veteran and a rape victim experience the same symptoms? The simple answer is 'Yes' and 'No.' So not a simple answer really. All victims will experience multiple symptoms that are discussed in the next chapter. Each reaction has a unique complexion. For instance, a war veteran is often haunted by the atrocities they have had to witness which they have not been able to prevent. They are also haunted by atrocious acts that they have been forced to do in the line of duty. They can often be overwhelmed with guilt for both of these reasons. A rape victim may be overwhelmed by feeling they have done something to deserve it. Women particularly will often blame themselves for the clothes they chose or the route home they took. The complexion of every story is distinctive, and it will be a collection of many of the symptoms explained in the next chapter. The experience is a collection of all that the incident produced and what the person brought to the incident from within their own life history. A perfect example of this is assault. Assault by a stranger may cause us to be hyper-vigilant on the streets and fear strangers for a while. An assault by a friend or family member brings into question that bond that is expected to be trustworthy. Betrayal by a loved one can be experienced as a loss of faith in everyone you know and everyone you don't know at the same time. The features of burnout and breakdown and how we might go about labelling them (so we understand them) are, however, the same. For instance, anxiety is a way of describing something, but we might not all experience it exactly the same way, equally depression, or headache. No two burnouts or breakdowns, then, can be exactly the same, even if they carry similar features. This is discussed more fully in the next chapter.

Untreated burnout and breakdown

Burnout and breakdown are the complete desolation after a trauma or build-up of stresses. Almost everyone will recover to some extent overtime, but if you've hit the bottom, recovery needs to be fast, thorough, and forever. If recovery is not thorough, it can lead to 'inelastic scar-like tissue' that builds up over your emotional wounding to protect you from the pain of it. That build-up of scar-like tissue then protrudes, and impinges on your life: for example, a victim of rape, where there has been no full recovery may subconsciously decide that they cannot have relationships as they are unable to allow themselves to be vulnerable. Equally, a man that has been accused of a rape left to deal with the accusation decides to stay away from meaningful relationships for the rest of his life.

Someone who has been involved in a car accident may never drive again. Someone who has experienced a near drowning doesn't go near water ever again. Our world is full with people who are in post-trauma aftermath, and we just accept it as a matter of course. Most families will have a story where they have a relative who does not do something or who always does something to avoid reminders and symptoms. This doesn't always have to be bad or difficult, but actually where it's life inhibiting it's an issue. We all have bits of experience that to a greater or lesser extent we've 'recovered' from. The difference in devastating events is that, yes, when it's not a thorough recovery it tends to come and 'bite' us in the future, requiring us to pay proper attention to our experience.

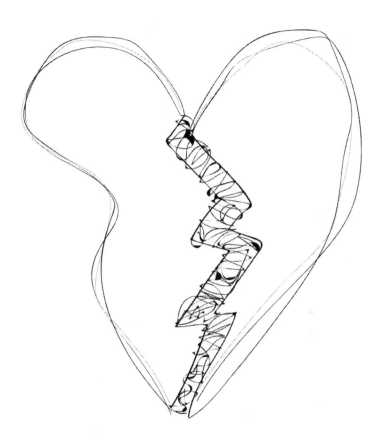

This image suggests that the 'heart and soul' of
a person is knocked out of shape and an
'inelastic scar' has built over the wounding so
they can carry on through life.

'The best has been done to help the heart
mend and cover the 'breakage,' though the

protection is thick, the break can still be seen and felt with some associated pain or suppressed agony.'

If you fully recover, the bad things will always have happened to you, but it will become a 'smooth scar.' It becomes a memory, and it adds to your knowledge and skillskit for the rest of your life. This means that you truly heal, and with every bit you manage to heal, it becomes a new and strengthened resource with which to live your life. Your self-knowledge grows to a level where you can rely on your own guidance. You get a chance to develop through to the other side of the overwhelming stress and move to better times. Thorough recovery and a full skillskit mean the breakdown doesn't impinge and intrude on the things that you need and want to do; in fact, it becomes an energizer and motivator for your chosen life path.

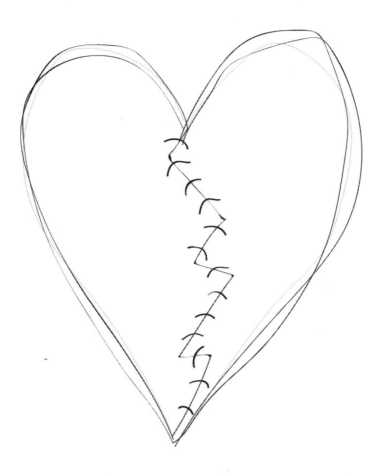

The heart is returned to its pre-broken state/shape. The scar is neat and can be seen and felt without associated pain. The scar is flexible and can move with the challenges of your life. It doesn't impinge, it is just there.

Numbing and illness

In the event of untreated trauma, your mind has an amazing capacity to protect you from the stuff that hurts and the stuff that gets in the way of your daily functioning. Your brain has a way of finding new pathways to living with its 'injury.' This works very well until it doesn't anymore.

The other way you may find you can cope is by numbing yourself from the horror of the symptoms. Once again, this works at some level until it doesn't anymore. This is known as psychic numbing; it's a clever way that we learn when emotional pain is overwhelming.

The abandonment of your ability to fully experience your real responses can lead to other difficulties, including other mental health and physical health issues. If you don't pay attention to what's happening, you will be unable to seek support and guidance through to recovery; you may find yourself numb and unable to interpret what truly is going on. The numbing of your experience is more than simply ignoring it or putting it aside for a while: it is a purposeful act of the mind to manage intolerable intense emotion. It's not your fault; it is, in fact, a clever adaption to difficult times.

It can start out as a clever way of managing an environment of constant reminders of terrifying times but that it mutates to go on to withhold you from life. It then goes on to cause you further harm as the numbing becomes so thorough that in the end, it reduces your ability to look after yourself and to fully function and fulfil your potential.

Example: A victim of gang rape numbed herself to the horrors of her experience and then became dissociated from her own needs for comfort from others. Victims go on to appear not to care about themselves, almost detached, the kind of person you might think 'you never really get to know the real her.' It's a clever but inhibiting mechanism in the long term. Whilst the mechanism works to protect us from further agony and threat at first, life isn't without further challenges. Life will inevitably bring new things to be dealt with, and this can be far harder if we haven't recovered and healed from previous hurts.

Part of thorough recovery is using the opportunity to discover and assemble the unique adaptation that has brought you to this point. Within post-breakdown treatment, it is possible to develop new ways of being by training the brain to create new neural pathways. This is known as neuroplasticity. For you here, it is your friend. Those things about you and those ways of thinking that you think are 'written in stone' are not. They are written into brain tissue which is soft, can be influenced and, therefore, changed. How cool to know that 'you can teach an old dog new tricks!' Seriously, though, this is great news for people who are on a path to recovery; with guidance, you can find new ways of being, believing, thinking, and feeling, which helps to keep you healthy and functioning at a level that is acceptable and enriching for you. This is the case, no matter how 'set in your ways' you believe yourself to be. I have heard so many stories from the most 'entrenched minds' that they are convinced that a lot of their way of being is immovable and unchangeable, only to observe the most dramatic of changes towards fulfilment and happiness.

Example: The man who felt that he had to continue to work in his business for 60 hours a week or he wouldn't be respected or would fall behind competitors. He was absolutely resolute this was the case. With exploration, he could 'practice' not being there for 60 hours, taking breaks to eat, and to rest, and to think and to feel. He had felt he'd needed to be in control of his workforce but realised he was being unnecessarily controlling and not delegating, which meant he wasn't asking his staff to do what he was paying them to do. He had felt he must be there to watch and oversee. Overlook and oversee are great terms which suggest too much looking and seeing, and not enough trusting. The outcome being that when asking him to practice 'stepping back,' he was able to see it all ran just as smoothly, and his good management had helped achieve this. By practising doing differently, his whole system, mind and body got feedback that it was all OK, and began making new brain pathways to consolidate this learning.

Chapter summary

Feelings can't be wrong

Two types of traumatic burnout and breakdown:

- Type I: No time to prepare
- Type II: Slow to build

Every reaction has a unique complexion

Recovery with compassion is quickest

Blame, Shame & Judgement prolong recovery

Have faith you'll recover

Nothing is lost; it all becomes your skillskit for life

Get help sooner rather than later

You will recover

Process 1:
KNOWLEDGE – STRESS is CRAZY, you are NOT – gather knowledge about what's happening to you

My belief is that feeling better fast is, first of all, gathering the information you need to know about what's happening. Everybody goes through the same process. You might go through it more slowly or more quickly, but also, every single element of it is different for everyone. I do think the process is the same, though. It's worth mentioning here that because burnout and breakdown 'scramble' your mind for a while because of the sheer neurological overload, the stages will bounce around in an extraordinary fashion for most people.

The seven processes to feeling better fast become part of your skillskit for life. For instance, one of the things you immediately have to do with anybody who's traumatised, it doesn't matter from which path they've come to it, is to assist them in feeling safe again. Once you have experienced being able to find safety and even conjure up images of safety, this will never be forgotten and will go on to become part of your 'skillskit for life.'

With big life events like this, symptoms come as a consequence of the disarray and because the BRAIN DOESN'T KNOW THAT THE TRAUMA IS OVER, so the brain keeps telling the mind and the body that it's still in danger. Your primary aim is to gather the information about what's happening and why it's happening, helping yourself reach feeling safe and getting on to a trajectory of recovery.

You can also experience further stressful events and further adversity. The early stages of recovery need to be as simple steps as possible so to avoid further stress. Further stress and events known as secondary stressors are separate experiences away from the initial burnout. You may find that the mechanisms for moderating your reactions are out of kilter, and this is because the shock still needs you to take care of yourself and reduce further stress. You may find that a frightening but not endangering event will be perceived as a threat and you will 'jump out of your skin.' It is tremendously important to be mindful of the things you choose to do early in recovery and the kinds of things the people caring for you expect of you too.

If you can't feel safe or understand what's going on (that it's a normal reaction to an extraordinary event), then you can't move to the next process which would be looking after yourself.

Example: I have worked with people where just because they've experienced a sudden trauma doesn't mean that they won't be in a train accident. That would be unfortunate, but it doesn't stop us being susceptible. That person will have some knowledge; it won't stop them from getting symptoms, but they'll go back to finding out what's happening, safety, self-care, etc.

So, if you've been through a burnout and breakdown and you're beginning to get some handle on your way through, and something happens again that is shocking, you will need to re-establish your safety, look after yourself, and allow your true feelings to come out.

Example: A woman was witness to an armed robbery and has been extremely traumatised by being held under threat for 20 minutes, then has to face the assailant in a court case. This is another stressful event now experienced as completely overwhelming due to already being under-resourced by the stress of the robbery experience and then facing the court and assailants. Often court systems are aware of this, knowing that witnesses faced with the people who threatened their life will be prevented from giving good evidence due to fear and re-triggering of the original trauma, and so they provide screening, whether around the accused or the witness/victim.

Another useful example of witness traumatisation is that of jury members who are often subjected to repeated accounts of horrific stories and also atrocities done by one human being to another. This largely goes undetected, and jury members can find themselves feeling anxious, having intrusive thoughts of the case and other symptoms synonymous with post-trauma reactions. Again, these witnesses cannot mobilise and walk around to help their bodies cope with stress hormones, and there is so little they can do to prevent their minds reacting to the accounts they must hear. This is known as 'vicarious traumatisation' and is common in careers like the police, armed forces, social work, nurses, doctors, paramedics, lawyers, and judges. It's in these positions that slow-to-build burnout and breakdown can be a potential hazard. Difficult-to-see-and-hear material is commonplace and self-care should be a top priority. As everyone without fail has a limit, self-care and organisational care via human resources are required to keep people from being overwhelmed and remaining well.

Slow-to-build breakdowns; burnout

Before we go on to look at the characteristics of healthy recovery, it is useful to spend some time acknowledging the complexity of slow-to-build breakdowns. Once again, this truly is a subject that could be a whole discussion in itself, but I want to make some attempt to honour it within this text, even if I cannot do it full justice.

Slow-to-build-up burnout and breakdown can be incredibly complicated and demoralising. As stated before, each pattern of burnout and breakdown is as unique as a fingerprint. The important thing is to make the distinction between two types of breakdown. Slow-to-build breakdowns can be characterised two ways, I believe: one is where there is a long history of mainly different types of manageable stressors (i.e. if they were to happen in isolation they would not create breakdown). This may take shape in the form of a bereavement, redundancy, financial problems, and then something that forces through your limitations and causes rupture to your coping mechanisms and overwhelms you, prompting the burnout or breakdown. For you, it can be intolerably distressing and undignified to feel as though you have no real reason or no 'acceptable' reason to warrant the complete and utter desolation you are now experiencing. For you, it is crucial that you are helped to understand that you have not brought this upon yourself. It is absolutely possible to discover the pattern of stresses that have built up and have surpassed your limits of stress.

Secondly, the other avenue in slow-to-build-up breakdown can be where you have been emotionally and psychologically injured within childhood. This basically means that through no fault of your own you have for many years been functioning with a skillskit that was never allowed to be fully equipped. Early emotional and psychological injuries can affect your ability to develop into the person you want to be and have the life you dream of. It can even affect your ability to dream and have vision at all. We are all at the mercy of our early templates. If you have an early template with trauma within it, you may have a vulnerability that can cause debilitation many years after your childhood. Single shocks in adulthood that are Type 1 (unanticipated traumas), can reignite your early childhood trauma experiences. It is possible that this is an opportunity to develop yourself in the direction that you desire in order to be free of something that might be privately shackling you, and for you to release your creativity and new dreams. Slow-to-build-up burnout and breakdown can take longer to recover from, that's simply because of the length of time it has taken you to be fully adapted to your earlier experience. It may take a little while for you to find your pathway through to recovery when such sophisticated adaptations have been made.

Characteristics of slow-to-build-up burnout and breakdown tend to be the astonishing ability to live with and not to pay attention to emotional pain. For those of you who recognise this it is important to illuminate that no emotion lasts forever. If emotions are permitted - in other words felt and moved through - they simply go through you or wash over you; they do not last. It's only when you persistently label a feeling with judgements and attach meaning to feelings that they last and become 'sticky.' On an energetic level, this can mean that you have an internal juggling of emotion that you are trying to avoid. You have cleverly made (by accident or design) your own internal emotional 'minefield.' What a precarious and dangerous place for you to reside! This is totally normal and not your fault; it's what we're taught to do. As I was saying before, if you reside in such a difficult emotional place, you suffer, i.e. , you cannot focus on the things that are good for you, and you have adapted to believe all you can do now is to 'click off' to the intolerable turmoil and numb it.

All of the processes I include in this book apply to all people in burnout and breakdown, no matter what avenue they were thrown into it from.

You will need to gain enough knowledge to understand that you are not crazy, losing your mind, or mad. You need enough information to reduce your fear levels and your fear of the unknown. It is a crucial part of your recovery. As well as finding out for yourself through books and the internet, ask friends and family to help with some of the 'leg work' by making it easy to understand.

The old adage 'information is power' is somewhat

true, but it can feel a little scary or actually a lot scary when you first start looking into what is happening and why. What I want you to remember as you dip in and out of this book is that you **absolutely can recover**. Information is power if the information is paving the way to your recovery, but it is important not to overwhelm yourself. Knowledge can be increased a little bit at a time so that it actually becomes part of the solution for you and not part of the problem.

Information is a soother, like pouring cool water over heat. It soothes the system as you begin to truly understand you are having an ordinary reaction to an extraordinary event or series of stresses. During and after devastating events, the system is flooded with stress chemicals, commonly known ones being adrenaline and cortisol. Imagine you've had to do an emergency stop in your car and that rush of adrenaline that makes you frightened, blush, gasp, short of breath, tingle and then agitated is happening all the time. That's what it's like, but all the time, night and day. Imagine, for example, the 'rush of adrenaline' we can get when we're about to address a room of 500 people; we can feel the 'rush' which helps you prepare and do the best job possible. In small doses, this is vital in life; we know that. That's the feeling that you're dealing with all the time, for the moment. Knowledge can't stop the feeling, but initially reducing fear is a priority so that we can start to break the cycle of consistent releasing of adrenaline and cortisol.

'So, it's imperative that you know what is happening even if you don't know what to do to stop it or can't stop it.'

What is burnout, breakdown, and overwhelming stress?

I feel that it is useful for you to think about it in terms of trauma. You probably won't consider your experience as traumatic until you've seen the list of symptoms.

'Trauma is when you have a single event that's so incredibly shocking to all senses; it's completely and utterly overwhelming, and if something's happened in your life that isn't overwhelming, it isn't trauma. It's really helpful to people who are traumatised to know that that's the very nature of it: it is overwhelming to all senses, in all areas of prior gained resources and resiliencies.'

'Trauma can also be chronic, i.e., it can be a slow

build up of stresses where the body and mind cope with each stress one at a time. Each experience leaves a residual effect. As more and more stresses build, the person is incrementally weakened. This finally can culminate in a traumatic breakdown. So, it's not a one off overwhelming event; it's a build up of events and experiences that can finally overwhelm all prior gained resources and resiliences.'

What kinds of things are traumatic, and may result in burnout, breakdown, stress?

Bereavement and traumatic bereavement (e. g. murder, suicide, accident)

Diagnosis with critical illness

Domestic abuse (being controlled, berated, belittled, and physically assaulted by a partner)

Sudden relationship breakdown/Divorce

Bankruptcy

Assault

Sexual assault

Accidents

Natural disasters

Childhood traumas

Then professionally you could be the victim of:

Fraud

Assault

Sexual assault

Redundancy

Bullying

Media attack

Defamation of character

Witness to crime, or accident

Can there also be an overlap between personal and professional in the fact that personal trauma may lead to a professional trauma?

There certainly could, because, for instance, if somebody who is a well-known public figure has a relationship breakdown, that's a traumatic event for them, but it's also something that's in the public eye. It is all over the media, on television, radio, and newspapers or even in social media. It's almost like double the trauma because something that personally happened behind closed doors is actually now all over the newspapers, and we don't go a week without seeing a new victim of that. Similarly, if you are suspended from work due to an allegation, your reputation is sullied in front of others and can be irreparable.

Burnout and breakdown doesn't exist in isolation within one person – it affects the whole family

It affects your whole family system and its functioning. Immediate family living with you in the same home can be noticeably affected. Family members can 'feel it for you.' They sympathise and empathise and worry for you too.

This can have considerable impact upon children, for example, where they witness perhaps their parent or sibling going through traumatic breakdown. On the other hand (the gift, if there ever is to be one, is that), these same children witness a loved one going through something incredibly traumatic and recover. Indeed, it often turns out that parents are aware of this, and this can be a great source of inspiration to recover for their children and with their children. Obviously, there is some grief in facing the lost 'healthy' time with their children. The complexion of burnout and breakdown is so engulfing, however, the human spirit tends to find something to rise beyond the regret and finds inspirational courage to move to better times.

Families as a whole can often feel many of the symptoms that I describe in this book. That is because their view of the world has been altered dramatically too. Their reality is also altered. If the person going through burnout and breakdown is a parent, the authority within the home can change. This can be down to simply the person who does the cooking not cooking anymore or the person who does the cuddles not feeling like cuddling anymore (for the time being). It is normal for all family members to be afraid and worry that recovery is not possible. This too is understood by the victim of burnout and breakdown and can often compound their feelings of guilt. These feelings, however normal, hinder your ability to see beyond the now. It is necessary and useful for any family members to learn the processes that are likely to be faced after such devastating breakdown. This helps their own fears and feelings of helplessness and also mobilises them to be part of your recovery journey to getting fully well.

Family reaction to crime

This is particularly difficult for victims of crime who have to bear the total emotional and physical effect of the traumatic event, often with the perpetrator walking free without punishment. 'Lack of justice' becomes a huge issue for families after trauma, and it may be the case for your family too. Aggression and anger can be central to the 'traumatised family.' Whilst your family is thrown into disarray, the perpetrator walks free. This can cause rage against the perpetrator and system as a whole because you do not feel safe whilst the person is at large, and anger for the fact that the perpetrator is not punished adequately. This can engender great tension within the family, and of course, sorrow. It is important that your family understands that they will react to injustice. There is plenty of injustice in our world. It is important to honour the high level of stress and energy that courses through people in these circumstances.

To recap the two different types of trauma:

1. No time to see it coming

The first type is also called 'Unanticipated trauma,' which really means you have no time to get ready for it happening, so that will be things like accidents, natural disasters, assault, rape, for instance. There's no time whatsoever to plan an escape or to even steel yourself for what's coming. If somebody were to say 'there's a bomb going to go off in 30 seconds outside this building' we would have time enough to do some psychological preparation. Without any preparation whatsoever, it's massively more traumatic.

2. You can see it coming time after time, but can't stop it

The other type 2 trauma is also known as 'Anticipated trauma.' It means what it says. It is anticipated, i.e. expected. This includes all types of childhood abuse; it also includes bullying at work, domestic abuse where there's a kind of a sickening anticipation of when the next bad thing is going to happen to you. It particularly attacks the person's self-esteem, their perception, and often leads to asking themselves questions like:

'Am I bad?'

'Is it me?'

'Do I make them this way?'

'What is it about me?'

For those where there has been a prolonged 'drip-drip' steady and insidious build-up of stresses where three, four, five or more things have happened to them, it's as though they can deal with each one as they come along and then suddenly 'OVERLOAD', like the overload is a shock in itself. Many people have described to me taking each hit of something happening and then suddenly the body and mind says 'no more.' This is what I call the 'sliding down the back of the door moment' like you see in films. You've held it together one time too many, and 'boom' you close the door on the facade and you slide down the back of the door. You'll recognize this if you've done it; it doesn't have to be a door, it can be a wall, inside or outside, a fence, a car, anything you can slide down! Your legs buckle, 'the façade is over.' At this moment, you are experiencing a traumatic incident. The experience of a complete overload of the mind and body is traumatic in its very nature. To get to your limit, the end of your tether, the end of your rope, fuse, whatever you call it, is the experience of the utter breakdown of every strength, tool, pretence you have used until that moment. In the cases where it might be a redundancy or maybe a relationship break-up, none of those things on their own would be technically considered traumatic, but the build-up of those four or five things can suddenly cause a traumatic breakdown. Remember every single person has their limit. If it just becomes too much, it's because you've reached your limit, no judgement about it, it's as it is, and now you are faced with having to take care of you and getting better.

It doesn't matter how successful people are or how their lives are; everyone can have their fill. So for those who have had a build-up, and who've had no help along the way, they suddenly can become overwhelmed because they literally cannot take any more. For very successful people, that 'climb' down or that 'shove' into this turmoil is excruciating and often compounded by the critical public eye.

Are some shocks worse than others?

Some are worse, but there is no hierarchy. In the trauma field, it's common knowledge that there are six influences to how injurious a traumatic event can be. These are:

- Time spent experiencing the shocking event

- Severity of the event

- Ability to mobilise to help or call for help

- People coming to help

- Personal nature of the event i.e. hurt by a relative or in intimate relationship

- The public witnessing/humiliation of the event

Time spent in the shocking event

The time you're in the event is significant to how your burnout and breakdown may manifest. For instance, if you've been kidnapped and you've been held away for a week, that's massively more influential to the post-traumatic stress picture than if you were held for an hour. Equally, if you are in a car accident, and you are trapped in the wreckage for several hours, this is much more influential on the severity of your post burnout and breakdown than if you were able to get out and walk away within minutes.

So the length of time a person is terrorised for is influential to the aftermath in terms of severity of symptoms. On the whole, we like to be able to get out of the danger. This influences stress chemicals and helps the body manage the onslaught of adrenaline and cortisol. If we are trapped, there is no movement or ability to 'flight' to manage this drenching; it can be unbearable. If you can't move through the stress or shake off the effects of stress chemicals, it's paralysing, terrifying, and overwhelming.

Severity of the event

The severity of the injury is also crucial to the post-burnout and breakdown landscape. If someone was raped, and they were also physically injured during the attack, they would also be dealing with lifelong physical injury, even if they recover and are left with scarring alone. So, the physical body being left with injury and change influences how severe the symptoms are. In other words, there are physical scars and psychological scars to recover from.

Early avoidance of triggers is a common reaction. This is intensified if you carry a physical scar. The scar becomes the trigger in itself, i.e. you're being consistently reminded of the attack, and you struggle to find respite from it. Specialist attention is required. In my experience, this must be transformed into a mark of survival and strength, however impossible that is to believe in the early days. Physical injury is discussed later.

Ability to mobilise to help or call for help

Your ability to get help and to get out of the situation is an enormous indicator of how difficult the post-traumatic stress symptoms will be.

Example: Somebody's had a climbing accident; they've fallen off the side of a cliff, but they have broken both legs, so they're stuck and can't go get help. They're stuck, whereas for somebody who can manage to walk and finds help, their post-traumatic stress reaction will be different.

A person in a car accident who is trapped in the wreckage of the car is far more likely to develop post-traumatic symptoms and go on to experience traumatic breakdown. This is due to the overwhelming experience of being in a life-threatening situation for an extended period instead of seconds. Most traumatic incidents are experienced as near-death experiences. Often we would have fleeting experiences of such things, i.e. having to do an emergency stop and the rush of adrenalin that comes with that or crossing the road and being narrowly missed by a car. Those are almost like brushes with trauma. Burnout and breakdown would rarely be triggered by such events unless there was previous history that became reawakened due to the recent 'brush' with death. The person in the car accident who can open the car door and walk away from the wreckage has a better chance of a speedy recovery than the person who is trapped for some time. Not that the recovery is easy, it's just different.

Any type of entrapment floods the mind and body with terrifying chemical, psychological, and emotional sensations which are in turn experienced with great fear themselves.

Example: Having worked with a witness to a murder, he told me that the speed at which his heart was racing made him think he was going to have a heart attack. His fear then escalated at the thought of that, and then he truly thought he was going to die at that moment. He believed his heart could not cope with the speed it was going, and this was to end his life as well.

Indeed, for you to be traumatised, you don't have to be involved in the incident itself. You can be overwhelmed by being the witness to frightening experiences; to traumatic events. There is a significant difficulty with being a witness to a traumatic event, and that is a little bit like being the person who is trapped where you cannot mobilise to help yourself or others. When you witness terrifying events, you can be frozen to the spot; for instance, if you saw somebody wielding a gun, and someone was being shot. It is common for you to freeze under the intensity of the stress chemicals that are flooding through you. The experience of being unable to help the victim or call for help because you literally cannot move coupled with the sensation of the full intensity of the distress, renders the witness often in a worse state than the direct victim. The ability to mobilise actually helps your mind and body manage the flooding of the adrenaline and cortisol and other neurochemicals. As stated before, being able to help oneself within the trauma or to help others can ease, to some degree, the full onslaught of post-trauma experience.

People coming to help

Passers-by coming to help you will alter the severity of your experience. You will often recall situations where you were either ignored in their hour of need (which is deeply distressing and significant), or you recall the person who came to help. This dramatically changes your perception of people and 'restores' your faith in humanity. If you are hurt by another and people are bystanders and no one helps you, the common reaction is to lose faith in your fellow human. If someone witnesses it and comes to your aid, your faith in others is somewhat restored, or at the very least in balance. If you have been suffering under extraordinary pressure at work and you have sought help with workplace stress but were ignored, you'll find the pressure is compounded. This can leave you feeling more vulnerable and demoralised. If you have a boss or colleagues who have empathy and support you to reduce stress and feel better, you are less likely to burnout.

When you are the victim of burnout and breakdown, you will be able to vividly remember (if conscious) the person that came to help you even down to what they were wearing, what they said, and even their name. To experience your own vulnerability fully and find that someone comes to help you in that place, even if they just sit with you and talk gently to you, has an immediate soothing effect.

The other side to this is where you may later become embarrassed or ashamed of being seen at your most vulnerable. You will find that this lasts not as long, once you understand that on the whole, people want to help another.

Personal nature of the event

There are some incidents that 'cut deep' in a different way. If you are traumatised by someone who is supposed to be looking after you, the shock is different and has a deep impact. This is because to trust means you must be vulnerable. Vulnerability is necessary to build relationships; if it is then broken dramatically, it is powerfully injurious to you. We find abuse by mothers abhorrent in a way we don't with fathers; this is because abuse by mothers is by the very person who is primarily there to protect and nurture you.

In instances of domestic abuse, there is a subtle distortion of the intimacy built within the relationship that is dramatically broken and leads to slow-to-build post-traumatic stress. As well as the relational aspect, there is also the breaking of one's bodily integrity and often dignity. Male and female victims of rape, for example, experience extreme violation which consequently shapes their post-trauma reaction. You cannot be violated without feeling degraded; sadly they go hand-in-hand. Degradation such as abuse, rape, torture, and bullying can only have its effect and injure because of it being an atrocity upon one human being by another. This leads us to the next thing that shapes our post-traumatic reaction and our post-traumatic breakdown.

The public witnessing & the humiliation of the event

If you think about it, we're all way more comfortable if the thing that has happened to us went on behind closed doors. If we trip over something at home, we might feel a little daft, but we can brush ourselves down, our inner pride a little dented. If we trip over something on the street in front of a dozen people, we feel it differently. Some of us might be mortified to have witnesses to our little accident.

Let's think about how this might feel if we are assaulted by a family member. We will feel absolutely dreadful, but at least it's private; it's something we can 'dig deep' and deal with privately. Now let's think what it might be like if a partner of ours assaults us in front of witnesses on the street. That's a very different scenario; it's humiliating, degrading, and also includes the element, 'do people come to help?'

This is all made so much worse because in the first instance a little daft accident becomes front page news – for example, Neil Kinnock falling on the beach. In the second scenario, an assault by a loved one in public in front of perhaps a dozen witnesses becomes front page news in front of millions.

Example: Consider the cruelty of how the media treated Nigella Lawson: to have been assaulted whilst someone looks on, photographs it and doesn't even help , only to go on to sell the images to a mass media furore. Similarly, with Halle Berry: the treatment of personal affairs becoming public; leaked information, leaked photographs, a tragic and damaging loss of trust, a further attack to withstand.

So, the original event or tragedy is bad enough but now doubly difficult and made demonstrably worse by the media coverage. The reason that this 'hurts' the person so much and changes the nature of the burnout and breakdown is because we all care about what people think but mostly we care how others treat us. We care that people are considerate if we are suddenly vulnerable, and we need time to recover our personal strength.

When it is publicly demonstrated that we will not be supported to recover in private, we are fairly sure that a front page spread will affect our reputation and our livelihoods. It should never be underestimated the power that public humiliation can have in destroying the mental health, self-esteem, and livelihood of a person.

So, it matters to all of us what people think. If you were in an environment where you knew that people would feel sorry and come to your aid, you'd be encouraged. All of our evidence in this society as it stands is that there is a distinct possibility that some people will delight in your injury, or at the very least, do nothing to help.

That sounds awfully pessimistic, and of course, I'm generalising, but somebody who is amidst a burnout and breakdown can't pick out the specifics and often feel you will face your future terror with the worry that you will not be treated gently or well.

Example: Some victims I have worked with have often previously been the kind of people who have not been considerate or even kind towards injured people in the past. At times, they have even been mean-spirited towards them, and these very people who through no fault of their own become injured through freakish circumstances will be cognisant that others will judge them as they once did judge. It's like they project their own lack of empathy out on to others which then confirms their view back onto themselves. Therefore, convinced they are surrounded by people who won't care for them. Certainly, in the early days, their own lack of consideration is projected mainly onto themselves. You may often behave very punitively to others and at times be cruel towards yourself. Interestingly, these very same people later can reflect on their previous behaviour towards injured people and feel sorry for even their thoughts. They invariably go on to show acts of kindness towards the vulnerable/injured people, but of course, you might have guessed by now that I maintain that this compassion and kindness must first be felt towards themselves.

'Shame about that' – How vulnerability and shame shape your suffering

I was so close to naming this chapter 'shame,' but I knew if I did, no one would read it! I know I wouldn't. We've learned to stay away from such painful emotion. We don't want to read anything that is about to remind us or re-surface feelings of shame.

Although shame is a normal emotion, if you become overwhelmed by it, it is paralysing. It causes you to retreat, to punish yourself and to feel utterly distraught, which you may often need to suppress simply to cope with it. Suppressed shame over a long period can lead to depression, anxiety, unfulfilled dreams, potential, and lives. It saddens me that this is the case. Overwhelming shame causes paralysis of the psyche in order to protect you, and you will learn ways of suppressing it so that you can 'keep going' on a perfunctory basis.

The title of this is much more helpful and is something I want to say to you. Rather than the 'Shame on you' which in turn translates to 'shame on me,' I say to you, 'what a shame that happened to you.'

This is a significant shift that can be made for you to enter your road to recovery. Whilst shame is left 'unattended to,' it will fester away underneath the day-to-day goings-on. It will grow and breed lots of fabulous adaptations to help you deal with it. Our minds and bodies adapt beautifully around the shame; we will hide; we will stay small; we will keep secrets; we will develop anxiety; we will struggle to learn; we won't fulfil our potential and our dreams.

In 25 years of working with traumatised people, I have rarely come across someone who has wilfully brought trauma upon themselves. Almost never can I think of a time when the paralysis of overwhelming shame is warranted. That is not to say that I expect people not to feel it or that there is a magic cure. The feeling of shame is a necessary part of our 'full range of feelings' and our moral consciousness if you like. But it is so incredibly rare to work with people who have done anything that purposefully precipitated their breakdown. Yet there is hardly ever a time when no matter what the event or set of events is embarrassment and shame are not part of the reaction.

If you feel responsible for what has happened, whether that be the objective truth or not, it doesn't really matter; if you feel responsible, then that is when you can feel shame growing. In your mind, you feel it's entirely within proportion of your so-called 'crime' or responsibility. Whilst you are convinced of your responsibility in the early days after breakdown, you may feel shame growing exponentially, and this is exacerbated by your difficulty in pulling yourself out of your distraught state. You might learn to live with it, carrying it around like a dusty old suitcase; a dirty old secret, and though no one can see it, it corrodes you. In that place, you stay unfulfilled or hidden, even when you have so much to offer yourself and the world.

'I know that shame can be transformed into an energy that is so personally powerful that you will never be able to be 'knocked down' by another person or event in the same way ever again'

You can physically overwhelm shame and its hold on you. By that, I mean come to terms with the amount of energy that you are using to squash the shame down. If you were able to conceptualise that it is possible to use that energy for good in your life, you'd do it. Ask yourself, 'How does the shame serve me?' You'll find that initially, you have no control over it and that initially hiding kept you safe from further 'attack'. Later, it does the opposite; you start to feel ashamed that you're 'not over it yet.' 'How did I allow myself to get into this state?'And so the cycle continues.

The public nature of certain events is massively influential to your suffering after burnout, as is the humiliation and the associated personal nature of traumatising events; for example, in instances of work-related stress, domestic abuse, sexual assault, or rape. Those types of traumas tend to have stigma associated with them. You will feel this. It will feel tangible to you. If you are the victim, you are the victim. However difficult it is for you to get you head and your heart around, you did not set out for this to happen to you. Stigma or not, you can rise up and beyond it, and recover.

As well as blaming yourself for your frailty right now, you may be blaming and shaming yourself for not being able to get yourself better. If you're not used to reaching out for help, this can be excruciating. The best way to help someone who feels shame is not to feel it against them, i.e. , don't blame them for what's happened, not even secretly. People who feel shame will know that you blame them; they will be masters at spotting a genuine shame-free, blame-free person, and therefore, environment. It is this kind of environment and only this kind of environment where a person can feel safe enough to recover. I talk more about this in the chapter on Safety.

Are some people more likely to breakdown than others?

Yes, but only because they've had bad stuff happen to them already. The unfortunate thing about trauma and overwhelming stress is that it's like a revolving door. No matter how 'over it' you think you are, you are actually at the mercy of it.

The brain has an uncanny way of re-discovering events or re-enacting and reactivating the prior unhealed experiences in a primitive way of getting you to master it and recover completely and move on. In terms of survival of the fittest, it's the brain's way of saying:

'Take care now; pay the attention you need to towards these pains or the unhealed stuff will come back and insist you do.'

The other thing that really does compound the breakdown reaction is if there are any earlier events that are similar or that have caused some kind of vulnerability already. Shame from years before can be re-activated, if you like, by a more recent event. Unresolved shame makes you more vulnerable to traumatic breakdown. I would go so far as to say that anything unresolved from the past that is of significance will make us all more vulnerable, and or require us to face it again.

You might have a hunch that there is experience you haven't fully overcome from the past and hear yourself saying:

'I don't want to drag all that up again; I thought that was all in the past.'

The thing about shocking events is that they re-expose anything that is in any way similar (check out the bungee run effect later in the book). Totally unfair as that might seem; my belief is the brain and the body has a way of bringing it back to our attention. So you can see why people become so unwell and so defeated. They are not now only dealing with the accident they have just been through; they are now dealing with everything that feels, looks, sounds, smells similar from the past. The great thing is that you've more than likely found amazing skills, resources, and resilience in the face of these things in the past, and it is vital you can appreciate them and illuminate those skills, for use now, in the future, and for your future self-esteem and confidence.

What kinds of things might people experience after devastating events?

I have assembled a symptom list, which describes how you may feel after devastating events and how they might appear. You won't necessarily experience all from the list, but you will experience and recognise many of them. It's really important to me to state that this list is meant as a guide, to give you information to ease your suffering and to those caring for you whilst you're suffering.

If all we can do is help people understand their normal reaction to extraordinary events, then great. If people can see themselves or their loved ones in this place, then maybe they will get help and support to recover more quickly. As with the premise of this whole book, it's all about reducing suffering fast and thoroughly.

What are the symptoms?

I'm going to go through all of the symptoms that are well-known. Obviously, everyone can have a lot of symptoms that are unique to themselves, and that's what you've got to remember, but there is a list of very common symptoms. This is not meant to be prescriptive, but it is meant to be informative.

So, here is a list of symptoms in order of the most commonly seen.

- Flashbulb and flashback memories

- Hyper-vigilance & startle response

- Can't interpret physical or auditory stimuli

- Avoid all triggers

- Sleep problems: getting off to sleep, staying asleep, fitful sleep, nightmares

- Memory difficulties

- Neurological overload, retching, trembling

- Anxiety

- Shame

- Aggression towards self (in how you talk, meet & treat yourself)

- Guilt, including survivor guilt and witness guilt

- Revenge fantasies

- What if?

- If only?

- Why me? (turning it towards self)

- Despair

- Depressions

Intrusive thoughts & feelings we can't control – Flashback & Flashbulb

Intrusive re-experiencing is a very clinical way of saying things 'keep coming up, into your mind.' Some of these are like pictures– like a light flashing on and off. It might be a memory of an incident, of how you felt that flashes into your mind and goes as quickly as it's come; they are called flashbulb memory. These can be disturbing because they are so fleeting that you cannot predict when they are going to come up. It's very tricky because after a shock you need to know what is happening now and what is happening next. With flashbulb memories, you can't know that. You might find they are worse when a room is quiet. They are more frequent shortly after your overwhelming experience, and they are rapid, sometimes making you feel nauseous. It can be a lot like having motion sickness because of the speed of the images crossing the 'mind's eye.'

Then there are flashbacks, which is how we more commonly name both types of intrusive imagery. People often talk about having a flashback, but a true flashback is when you feel as though you are back in the event itself. In flashback, you can hear, smell, feel, see, and even taste all the same things from within the event. Your body and mind respond as though it is in the event or under attack. Flashbacks are terrifying and are experienced as a re-living of the events. You'll experience it as though it's actually happening right now. It means that the body and mind, in turn, become flooded with stress chemicals. Your body and mind respond to feeling unsafe again, and so the cycle continues. You may be able to see by now that there is a pattern of post-traumatic symptoms causing more re-occurring symptoms.

Example: For someone who's had the slow build-up and then a traumatic breakdown, they might actually have intrusive re-experiencing of the moment of the breakdown when they knew they 'couldn't do this anymore,' when they felt the rupture in their resources and resilience. People have told me graphically of the moment they knew the 'break' happened. People often recall a simple task that they could not perform; writing a shopping list, wrapping a present, making a meal.

The other thing about re-experiencing that's helpful for you to know is that those of us that burnout and breakdown are often the driven ones who work hard. These same people often don't stop to think and to feel, but because they have burnt out and are now experiencing breakdown, they have been forced to stop and pull out of life as they knew it for a while; this can be a frightening prospect. Their strength and ability to overcome stress and be able to operate under stress has gone for the time being.

Heightened vigilance and exaggerated startle response – Looking out for danger, so you don't get caught unawares – being 'jumpy'

In real life, what that actually means is somebody is walking down the street and because of what's happened to them, they feel incredibly vulnerable. This kind of person is walking down the street, and if for instance, they've been assaulted by somebody in a black suit, everybody with black suits seems scary to them, so it causes them to be overwhelmed and frightened. Hyper-vigilance is frantically looking around, your eyes darting from person to person, place to place. It's your brain's way of trying to keep you safe by anticipating another bad event. It's a very clever mechanism, but it's actually quite tiring. If an event has taken you unawares, and you have not had time to steel yourself against it and protect yourself from being utterly overwhelmed, the common reaction is that your brain will do its damnedest not to be caught unawares again.

Example: A client who had found an intruder in their home became pre-occupied with locking internal and external doors, which then went on to become an elaborate set of rituals initially all about being prepared and being safe. It's a protective mechanism against further threat; the problem with it and for the sufferer of it is that the brain doesn't know when to give up the defence, i.e. the rituals. The person can easily become exhausted, avoid situations where they might be 'triggered,' i.e. avoid all places where men in black suits may be seen.

Hyper-vigilance may also be seen in rituals a person may be doing for the first time since the shocking event. Clients after assault will lock doors, lock rooms, not allow their children out to play; with many different permutations of this as there are people. The trickiest triggers are those that are more generalised. An assault by a stranger in jeans can cause all men in jeans to become a trigger to a worsening of anxiety symptoms and fight-and-flight episodes. Avoiding people in jeans is incredibly difficult. Getting some help with this is vital if the symptom persists as it has often led to people staying at home and becoming agoraphobic.

When you have been engulfed by this neurological state, you may be hypersensitive to sound, touch, smell, taste, physical stimuli. You may react to the most bizarre stimuli with anger or aggression as you perceive it as a threat, because for now you have lost your ability to differentiate between threat and non-threat.

Inability to interpret physical and auditory stimuli

This inability to distinguish between stimuli causes great anguish, sometimes making you think you are continually unsafe, and so therefore you are continually afraid and so continually in the cycle of stress chemicals of adrenalin, cortisol, and other chemicals zooming through your system. This goes on to tell the brain that there is a threat when there is not. Imagine that you are constantly ready to face danger and the heart is racing; you're sweating, you're nauseous, you're irritable, and now you're weakened and tired by it as there is no respite from it. Only to find out that there was no threat anyway. It is a barrage of chaotic stimuli that causes further overwhelming as your brain has almost forgotten for a time how to 'freeze' out certain unnecessary bits of information. It's like every sense has become highly tuned and 'loud', just in the hope that it won't get caught unawares again.

This exaggerated startle to a response is a scientific, kind of clinical way of saying you're a bit jumpy. This symptom is where you 'jump out of your skin' if you hear a loud noise you didn't expect. If somebody says hello, and you didn't see them coming, you might 'jump out of your skin' and scream. You're already hyper-vigilant and rather overwhelmed; there is no ability to decipher what is a true threat, so cleverly the brain assumes everything is a threat in the strangest way to keep you protected and safe. You may see already that these odd and debilitating symptoms are the body's way of protecting you, however crazy they may seem.

Avoiding 'triggers', specific reminders of what's happened

'Triggers' are the name for anything that sets off a physiological and emotional reaction. They are most often associated with the original event or set of events that has precipitated the breakdown. This is not, however, necessarily always the case. It is useful for you to ascertain what triggers there are for you and how you might in the early days avoid them, and latterly how you might desensitise them. It's normal to spend a great deal of physical and emotional energy trying to avoid reminders of the event in an attempt to diminish emotion allied with it. The numbing, it appears, is necessary to bring about the dampening of the arousal symptoms and the emotional pain. Once again, you have made clever adaptations early on trying to alleviate some of your own sufferings. This is useful to remember when you may have times feeling despairing and helpless and hopeless. You can help yourself by seeing that there are intricate and intelligent adaptations you have made to survive the overwhelming experience.

Sleepless and fitful nights

Struggling to get off to sleep, stay asleep, and have restful sleep

No wonder really that after a great traumatic shock you'd struggle to sleep; the first two symptoms alone would make that difficult. Certainly, with any type of traumatic breakdown, you will struggle to sleep. You're very tired because of all the symptoms with the adrenalin and cortisol, chemicals running around their body and not being able to quiet the mind. Although you're tired, you will put your head on the pillow and then your mind will be racing at such a speed that it's impossible to get off to sleep. So you might find that you can only sleep an hour at a time. You might find you can sleep three hours in 24 hours. That contributes to lots of different difficulties, such as loss of concentration and memory as well as exhaustion.

Sleep disturbances also include nightmares.

It's very common to have nightmares, a bit like the re-experiencing above but during sleep. Sometimes you may actually wake up retching or being sick. It might be the first thing that happens when you wake up, as you are becoming conscious of what's happened anew each time you awake. It's not just about how much sleep you have; it's about having restful, restorative sleep. Lack of sleep and disturbing, terrifying nightmares only compound your anxiety and fret. There's a cruelty in not being able to sleep. You may long to sleep so you can literally escape from the torment and have some respite from the symptoms. This gets better with time, and as daytime gets easier, restful sleep will too.

Memory difficulties and recall – Loss of short-term memory whilst vivid memory of the event persists.

The sleep disturbances obviously affect your ability to concentrate, but most of you who are traumatised, particularly in breakdown, will have initially some short-term memory problems. You may unknowingly repeat yourself; you may not remember who you have seen in a day; you may not remember hour-to-hour, but your long-term memory may be crystal clear. Your short-term, hour-to-hour memory is scrambled initially, and this settles and gets better as external threat recedes. It's like your brain can't take anymore: it's overwhelmed and is now struggling to see the order of things. One of the major features of stress is a jumbling up of thinking, not being able to think sequentially, though you may find at the same time you are tormented by the sequence of events that brought you to now. So we have a situation where the memory is not in order. You may struggle to know whether you've eaten, who you have seen in one day, to know days of the week, whether you have brushed your teeth, how to get somewhere in the car or forgetting how you got there.

Neurological overload – Uncontrollable trembling

Your nervous system is overactive and over-stimulated, and it's also got so much adrenalin and cortisol running around, your body can literally shake from head to foot. In burnout and breakdown, you may have difficulty eating or going to the toilet as you normally would. You may struggle with solid food; you may have absolutely no appetite. You can lose a lot of weight as anxiety is continual. Waves of acute anxiety come in separate episodes to the constant low-level anxiety; these are extremely hard to cope with and knowing the episodes come and go often without any trigger can cause anxiety in itself. This can be one of the hardest symptoms to endure; especially when it is not something you have experienced before. Trying to eat small amounts to keep your blood sugar steady is helpful, can be tough but necessary to help stabilise you.

One of the offshoots to persistent anxiety, including the trembling, is the inability to function at a higher level of cognition. It can be tough to think things through. Inhibited ability to function, for some readers of this book, is one of the scariest symptoms. For those who are used to operating at a high cognitive level, for example in business, you face the reality of losing your businesses and your livelihood too. This further worsens your anxiety, and for some this is unbearable. Some who work and live in the public eye will face the reality of believing their burnout and breakdown will happen on a public stage. This can be construed as a witnessing of your demise. During this level of turmoil, it is impossible to convince you that you will come through this, survive it, and thrive again. Sadly, this is one of the symptoms and feelings that can often lead to suicidal thoughts and self-harm and even acting upon the suicidal thoughts. As I was saying before, everyone who has been through a catastrophic event or set of events will suffer incredibly. If we were to live in a world where people were supported quickly, effectively, and with compassion, there would be no need for this suffering to be lengthy and painful.

When you can't function in the way you need and want to, you will experience this as a loss and something to grieve (cry about). In the early stages, you cannot believe you will get your functioning back. I do know that it's possible to get your functioning back (if you have not suffered brain injury), but I cannot convince you of it right away.

Example: One of the things people say to me about losing their ability to function, no matter what level it is at, is that they don't recognise themselves anymore. For me, one of the major features of symptoms after catastrophic event/s is the cruelty of people losing their sense of self. The loss of the lives they'd lived. There is literally nothing that is untouched in their life. I've had clients who are used to running multi-million-pound businesses with thousands of staff or doing presentations to hundreds of people at a time, and of course, now they find themselves trembling, unable to sleep, and cannot leave home. The fear that this provokes becomes overwhelming in itself. This fear and the consequent overwhelm leads to furthering the cycle of anxiety. It's vital to support people in achieving the hope and vision that they will get back to their former selves or to their better selves no matter what.

Anxiety – Worries, fears, agitation

All of these symptoms cause anxiety in themselves, really, and that's important to remember. Anxiety on a consistent basis makes us behave in the most unusual ways. You may be aware you behaved in ways you never thought you would. Previously gregarious and spontaneous, you may find you suddenly don't want to go out at all. In some ways, this smaller life in the short term is useful, I feel. It allows your body some time to get some balance, to stay quiet and safe. So rather than hurting yourself with worry about not going out or not being able to perform at work, this 'lying low' for a while is not all bad. If you've had a slow to build up of stresses, you have been out of kilter for some time. This quiet is just what you need to create time to establish care for yourself and your recovery.

Build-up of shame and distrust – A natural reaction to events and to not being able to recover

The majority of people who burnout and breakdown are hard workers. You will most likely start to hold it against yourself that you cannot navigate your way to recovery. You can't pick yourself up and brush yourself down in the way you always have. Sometimes you'll find that shame comes from the type of event you have experienced, and too because you 'haven't got over it yet.' Shame becomes entrenched and can grow the longer it takes you to feel better. You may grow to understand that anybody can be the victim of traumatic events, but you may believe that you should be able to 'fix' yourself. The truth of the matter is that trauma is, by its very nature, overwhelming, and is incredibly difficult to recover on your own. Needing help is not a weakness, it's a vital step to not being alone with your symptoms and getting on the 'upward spiral' of recovery. Of course, asking for help is made all the harder now, whilst you distrust others and the world more.

The above symptoms are the most common and most likely you will be experiencing; below is another set of symptoms that you may experience after burnout and breakdown.

Aggression against yourself and others – Hitting, shouting, biting, cutting

Aggression against yourself and others is not always physical. It is sometimes through having a short fuse and angry outbursts. This is actually quite a common symptom in people who have broken down. For some, it is made worse by feeling stuck and feeling like you 'should be better by now.' If you've nearly always been the person who fixes things and helps other people, you may struggle with this 180-degree turn. A normal reaction to this is to feel weak and to be angry towards yourself. You might feel like harming yourself because the emotional agony is too much. This can often be a way of coping with extraordinary physical symptoms and the physical manifestation of emotional symptoms. It is to be taken very seriously, as this can lead to injury and attempts on your own life.

You might hurt yourself physically or you might drink to excess or use drugs to calm your symptoms down and to calm your cruelty towards yourself down. Everyone has their limit, including you. Your brain and your body can only take so much stress. It's okay to be angry, but when you turn the anger against yourself, you hurt yourself more. This is covered further in Head Pictures in the next chapter.

Guilt

Some people feel guilt about what's happened to them, whether they felt that they wore the wrong dress, whether they shouldn't have taken the bus, the taxi, or taken the challenge. They just can feel guilty for something they think they might have done to make the event or set of stresses happen. This is a very common symptom when trying to understand something that has so dramatically changed your own life.

Survivor guilt

Guilt can be experienced in a devastating fashion if you have been in an event with others where somebody did not survive but you did. This can be crippling and can cause an onslaught of 'what if' scenarios zooming through your mind's eye, and literally tormenting you. You can feel badly for feeling good that you have survived when someone else did not. You can also have profound guilt if you felt you should have done something to help the other person or people. This is a normal reaction that must be felt in order to process it. If you squash it down, it can lead to suppressed rage against yourself and can lead to adaptations that in the long run won't help you. Sometimes it is useful to look at the decisions you made about yourself at the time. Often you have convinced yourself of something that may have an alternative interpretation. It is good to be able to change your mind about something you have believed deeply.

Witness guilt

Witness guilt is felt mostly when you have witnessed someone being hurt and were not able to go and help. As a witness, you may feel frozen to the spot with fear by your own stress response to the overwhelming assault of neuro-chemicals. You can go on to develop extreme guilt that you stood by and watched someone be hurt or killed. Once again, this needs to be handled delicately. You would have helped if you could. Our bodies react in ways that prevent us from moving. Frozen with fear is a natural response to shock. Look after yourself; it is worth remembering to notice and gently send shame away so you can recover.

135

Revenge fantasies

Some people have revenge fantasies. Revenge fantasies are quite normal but can be quite disturbing for you. You might suddenly be having violent thoughts and want to 'rip someone's head off,' or you might find yourself plotting how you might create someone else's downfall. You might be rather perturbed by these symptoms, particularly if it is out of character for you. It's just the brain's way of creating justice and protecting you. It's completely normal, as long as you don't act upon them, which in turn will only make you less safe. Usually, if you allow a safe place to talk through this, write about it, or draw it, it's nothing more than that. Allow it, attend to it, honour it, and move through to recovery.

'What if?' scenarios

The brain starts throwing out 'what if?' For instance, if you had experienced a robbery, you could think, 'What if he'd had a knife?' 'What if he had a gun?' The brain almost can't help telling the alternative other story. Friends and family might say to you, 'Well, it could've been worse,' but your brain doesn't know that. Your brain is saying,

'Well, it actually could've been this.' It will torturously show you images of what the worst-case scenario would've been, even if that's already happened. It's just a strange way of the brain trying to get some control.

Example: I have had people literally draw out the vivid images that they think could have happened had the situation been worse. For instance, victims of assault and sexual assault can often have uncontrollable images of what might have happened had the assailant had a knife and used it. It's usually associated with the feeling of being close or narrowly missing death.

'If-only' scenarios

Kind of things you might say for example:

'If only I'd listened to my husband/wife.'

'If I'd not gone down that road that day...'

'If only I had gone the way I usually go.'

'If only I'd have taken that taxi at eight, the event wouldn't have happened at quarter past eight.'

'If only I had listened to my exhaustion.'

'If only I'd have got help sooner.'

'If only I had listened to my friends.'

It's not uncommon to be preoccupied with the 'If-only' scenarios. Many people blame themselves; indeed, many others will blame you also. You are trying to make sense of an array of symptoms that are really causing you to suffer on an hourly or even minute-to-minute basis. You are trying to gain some control over a completely out-of-control situation. It is a clever little mechanism of the brain actually. But unfortunately, it can be heavily related to guilt.

Example: This can be particularly significant in younger people, especially children if something happened when they were told by a parent not to be in a certain place.

A helpful way through this stage is to allow yourself to be kindly and caring about what has happened to you. Nobody intends to become traumatised or intends to traumatise themselves; if you did, you wouldn't be in such breakdown. This symptom or 'trail of thought' is often worsened by the feeling that you will be judged and blamed for what is happening to you, and so you feel guilt, shame, and so the cycle continues.

Why me?

Quite often, people will think 'Why me? What is it about me?'. It is helpful to tease out what you believe about yourself and what decisions you have made about yourself that you think made this happen to you. You may make rash judgements or decisions early on that can become entrenched and more difficult to shift. Here are some self-beliefs that can form in the self-doubt of 'Why me?'

'This happened because I'm weak.'

'Why me? I have always been good to others.'

'Why me? I've never hurt anyone.'

'Why me? I can't even look after myself.'

'I must be to blame.'

'Now I'll never be me.'

It makes sense for you to want to make sense of this. Early information about what is happening helps this. The main concern is to reduce the overstimulation of the nervous system and to help you feel safe again. Unsurprisingly, you want to cling to making sense of anything to gain control over this chaos. However, turning this against yourself can be hard to undo later on. No one truly consciously tries to break themselves down.

Preoccupation with death

Feeling close to death and facing death

Trauma in burnout and breakdown is overwhelming and forces you to face near-death experiences. No matter what your age, this can be terrifying and can change your outlook irrevocably. One of the other symptoms you experience is something that we call a 'foreshortened future' or fear of death.

If you've been in a catastrophic event or you've had a traumatic breakdown, you do suddenly feel mortal; you do feel vulnerable. It's very normal to feel that way. This is actually particularly poignant for children because if children aren't traumatised, they feel like they're going to live forever (and it has been called the loss of the 'shield of invincibility'), and it's shocking when they realise they won't or people don't. It's still very poignant for adults, no matter who you are, to understand it's normal and think, 'Oh gosh, what's going to happen; how can I survive this?

Am I going to recover?' This is a normal reaction. Burnout and breakdown can feel so intense that you may feel your body and mind can't survive it. You may be stunned that you've taken your health for granted until now, and this vulnerability feels alien to you.

Depression

Depression is a common reaction to both types of breakdown. If it is reactive depression, once again this is a clever way of your body surviving something that doesn't feel survivable. And in the short term, this most probably has no detrimental effect, but in the long term, suppression can lead to depression because ordinary emotions are not allowed or attended to. The ability to suppress can be energised and by denoting certain responses as inappropriate can make assumptions and decisions quickly in order to reduce our suffering. Suppressed feelings that are not understood may need to be understood or at least acknowledged to be let go of. Whilst your feelings are suppressed, they remain, and will require energy to be kept at bay. Rather like shame that grows as we turn our back to it, suppression does not diminish the size or the pain of the feeling, it simply keeps it locked in time within your body.

Example: Unfortunately, a person who has had to use suppression to get themselves through now feels depression as well. I am often introduced to people with depression, often via GPs, and it is not uncommon rather quickly to discover that the depression is a result of suppressed trauma. In some ways, once we can see the suffering for what it is and where it began, we can get a good handle on it, discover its pattern and discover the way out of it. If we consistently live in a place of suppression and in an environment where we are not nourished, our true selves are suppressed some more. Small steps with big gains can happen when we can see the pattern and take care and consideration of this un-nurtured self that lies within us.

Despair – Feeling overwhelmingly at the end of your tether

Despair is a good emotion to end this section on. If you can see that you or someone you know is experiencing the majority of the symptoms above all at one time, you can understand how this would lead to despair. People I have worked with over the years find the feeling of despair the most difficult to understand.

Despair backs you into a corner and leaves you nowhere else to go. When you are left alone with despair, this is when you will feel like hurting yourself or hurting others. Learning about despair, however difficult that subject is, has over the years provided me with an opportunity to help others understand what's happening to them.

The experience of despair is so incredibly traumatic in itself; we must as a community, as a culture and society, find ways of helping people when they are in that place. I know that someone can come back from the place of despair many times understanding that despair is despair and it's not a loss of mental health. Of course, if you are overwhelmed with these myriad symptoms, it's almost impossible to convince you that you can navigate the times of despair.

Example: If you're experiencing despair get help now. I say to people out loud that " I'm not going to try to convince you of this today and I know that I cannot convince you of this today, but there is a way through this and it won't be like this forever. " One of the major bonuses of working alongside someone who knows about trauma is that they can act as a guide to see you through these difficult experiences and through the despair. I've come full circle back to why I wrote this book in the first place, I want to reach out to you in an ordinary straightforward fashion in order to help in some way to aid understanding of a string of symptoms that are so overwhelming, which can lead to despair but that won't last.

Self-harm during despair

Earlier, I talked about metaphorically having the big stick, but actually I don't want to make light of how desperate you might feel. It is not uncommon for people who have been through such traumatic times to feel despair and hurt themselves. This can be in the form of biting, hitting, and cutting yourself, but also drinking excessively, taking prescription medication amongst other things in order to nullify the agony.

Example: People I have worked with talk about this as 'going into self-destruct.' It can often take the form of starving themselves, consuming medication they do not require or drinking large amounts of alcohol. People have described to me on many occasions that dealing with the hangover from copious amounts of alcohol is a distraction welcomed compared to their emotional turmoil. That is a measure of the acuteness of this post-traumatic state. To binge on alcohol, consuming perhaps the weekly recommended amount in a day is actually considered a better alternative to the symptoms themselves, that about sums up the level of distress you find yourself in. My heart goes out to people who feel this way. It is some reassurance that however 'out of control' these may seem, if we deal with the effects of the initial traumatic experience, we are well on the way to overcoming the addiction. If we do away with the 'hold' the trauma has on us, i.e. , it was trauma induced, we have the best chance of recovery from addiction too.

I think it's natural for you to want to grapple with and dampen down your neurological overload. Someone said to me once that feeling this devastated was like a constant feeling of trying to thread a needle and not being able to do it. I thought this was a perfect description of the intensity of overload where in the moment you can't thread the needle the frustration is of such a physical and psychological magnitude that your agitation is overwhelming. That is what burnout and breakdown are like all the time. The onslaught of feelings physiologically, emotionally and psychologically all whirling round together. No wonder then that you'd want to dampen that down, or feel like hurting yourself.

Dealing with this emotional and physiological intensity must not be underestimated. I have immense respect for anyone who has brought themselves through this.

Reaching out in the moment – the antidote to despair

One of the things that will help you in despairing moments is reaching out for support when you need it. It is crucial to share how you feel and not be alone with despair. I urge you to name it, to recognize it as despair. It can help; you know it won't last and can help you separate away from the panic that is felt within it. In other words, however frightening, it will pass, and it will pass more quickly if you are not on your own with it. Be genuine with how you feel with people you can trust. Isolation will worsen feelings of despair. So it becomes a vicious cycle. It doesn't have to be that way. Practising 'reaching out' when you need to is good for the soul, and it also helps you build support mechanisms around you. Often people want to help, but they just don't know how to help you. We tend not to reach out during despair because we feel so desperately vulnerable and weakened by it, but soon it can become an upward spiral and will speed up your recovery.

It is such a shame this is the case – in our world, with so much compassion and certainly the ability to show compassion, people still find themselves in this cycle. But again, this isn't about blame; this is about finding reasons and ways to improve a desperate situation. What we don't want to do is to engender an atmosphere of blame because people aren't reaching out. That defeats the object completely. What I say to believe is: we are just trying to find ways towards a healthy path to recovery. Blame is not helpful at this stage. Reasons are very useful because they illuminate the path to recovery. No matter how old the sets of symptoms look and feel, they are usually a remarkable attempt by the mind and body to look after you as a whole. That seems utterly ridiculous at first, I'm sure, but actually when you analyse the multitude of horrific symptoms, it makes some kind of sense.

Example: Many people I have worked with have become agoraphobic in the months following an initial shocking event. So, previously professional and entrepreneurial people find that they cannot leave the house. This makes complete sense to me because it's as though the organism is trying to protect itself from any further possibility of stress. I have told people how that makes complete sense. If you don't go out, you reduce the chance of being taken by surprise by bad stuff; what can happen in your living room? If you think about it, it's a really clever way of the mind and the body's whole system working together to reduce the possibility of further assault against the system (the mind and body). Interestingly when I share this with people, it can reduce their feelings of embarrassment and shame as they realise some space from their everyday life might be exactly what's needed in the short term.

Another useful thing for helping yourself with despair is consistently telling yourself that this is only for the time being, and it won't always be this way. Almost nothing stays the same; there will be a shift in your feelings of despair also. Another thing you may find helpful is to be helped with little tasks that you can do instead of hurting yourself; things like doing the complete opposite of what you feel. You feel like smashing yourself up, then go apply some make-up; you feel like you're going to smash your face, then go for a short walk. Make yourself something to eat; write something on a notepad. What your whole system will get feedback about is that now you're taking steps to be good to yourself when you least feel like it. Great! This will become the upward spiral; you're making friends with your despair. I know that sounds totally crazy, but I believe it. It's right that you've been through too much and had enough of this, but hurting yourself for being here is not helping in the long run. Why? Because when we start to feel bad about ourselves being in the breakdown itself, it's another form of hurting ourselves.

There is no blame and shame in having to learn this caring for yourself either. I want you to know that I care that you are hurting, and I care that you feel better as soon as possible. I know that small steps of self-care help to look after you and lay the path to recovery much quicker.

Gathering information when you are in despair

One of the threads of this book is the use of very simple images in communicating about what is happening to you, the symptoms, the different steps, and how you might get through them. I use images because when you're traumatised, you're ten times more likely to be able to understand because you can see images as well. If you're already overwhelmed, you are struggling with concentration; you are struggling with anxiety, so you don't take in information as well. If you draw it or see drawings, it's much easier to see it and take it in.

Chapter summary

You will recover – everything changes

There are many symptoms; you won't necessarily have all of them

Everyone's reaction is unique

It's crucial to be able to calm yourself down

Learning why you feel like hurting yourself

Reach out when in despair

Make friends with your despair; it's a sign of how deep the wounding is

Interlude:
STRESS hates you making headspace – MAKE MORE HEADSPACE!

How you observe what's happening is crucial to your recovery. It's so important that complex information is made receivable.

I've found simple ways of helping when you're struggling to be able to view information and be able to take in that information. I want to consistently help you to stay separate from what has happened to you and who you are as a person. In other words, who you are as a person is not what has happened to you. You are better equipped and arguably only equipped for recovery when you can separate yourself from the event or set of events. So, when I am literally drawing things out, it helps to normalise what feel like extraordinary reactions, and it gives you access to symbolic language as well as verbal. I'm showing you this head picture as I have discovered that it truly helps to understand the feeling of being overwhelmed.

Head Picture 1

The first head picture is one where there is 'space' in the person's mind (and body) to deal with the everyday challenges they face. If you have space, you can manage, tolerate, and cope with things you need to attend to. You have the space to have vision, to dream and do the things you want to and need to.

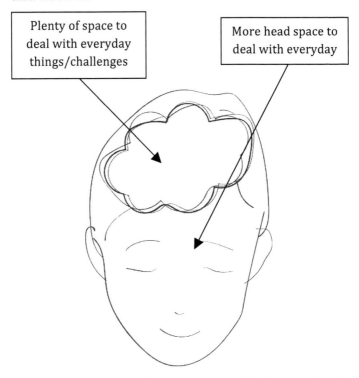

Plenty of space to deal with everyday things/challenges

More head space to deal with everyday

The two arrows are pointing to the 'everyday'

space that you have to deal with everyday issues and challenges. There is nothing encroaching on the space, on your resources. You feel resilient, capable, and strong.

Head Picture 2

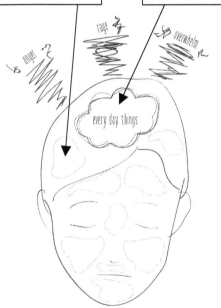

Lots of different 'sized' experiences; good and bad. Bad ones stored up filling the space to deal with every day.

Only this tiny space to deal with everyday challenges

In this simple image, the head (and body) can

be full of different-sized things which have become overwhelming. There becomes a much smaller space to deal with every day. The simplest of demands on you whilst in this state can then fill the space you have for every day. This can create 'overwhelm' and the consequent symptoms. The head is full and the smallest of demands can cause anger, rage, and overwhelming.

It's normal when you're overwhelmed by stress to have lots of different 'things' inside your head. Lots of memories of what has happened to you throughout your life. These things will be different shapes and sizes and have different meanings and different amounts of worry or distress attached to them. These things bother you a lot or a little. As they build up overtime without being processed and released along the way, overwhelm, burnout, and breakdown can be the result.

You can easily become irritated and further overwhelmed by another simple demand made upon you.

Example: If asked to do a simple task, this will go into the space; this will fill the little space that they had to deal with every day, so very quickly a traumatised person can become further overwhelmed because they had so little resources in the first place. The natural reaction to being overwhelmed and having too many demands made on you is to be angry, and this is good in a sense as it has energy. If it becomes too much, the simple demand can create a slump, the last straw, the burnout, the breakdown. People can find this very difficult to live with, out of character, and also loved ones can find this very frightening and unbearable.

You can try creating this diagram for yourself at home. You may find it illuminating to find out what the things are that are causing pressure. You may find that it helps to see that actually you've been through more than you thought. It might be that it shows you that there are some things worse than others. Big or small, those things may have now have become reactivated and troublesome. The image gives you something tangible to grapple with. By putting it on paper in image form, you take it out of yourself a little, and you don't have to spend energy 'holding the thoughts' together. If this helps you understand your anger, your breakdown, your despair, then that is a great step (most people I have worked with underestimate what they have been coping with).

Head Picture 3

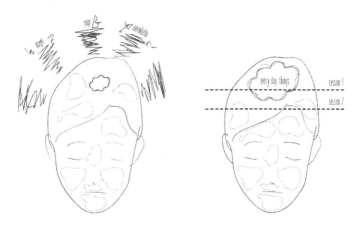

In this image, you're working to gain 'space.'
Working to achieve safety, and security and
self-care and so on means you are working all
the time to relieve the build-up of tension and
to provide 'feedback' that there is increasing
space and resources to deal with what is
happening.

In the image on the right, you see that space is
incrementally created by processing what has
happened to you, how you feel about it, how
you are affected, and how you feel about
yourself. As time goes by and especially with
help, you gain space every day. Each of the
things that you've been through is 'moved' to
memory and does not fill up your head space.

Head Picture 4

Traumatic things have become part of memory. This allows the rest of the space to enjoy fully and smile again.

Now your experiences are nicely placed in memory without causing you distress. You have all this space to deal with everyday challenges, and you can smile again.

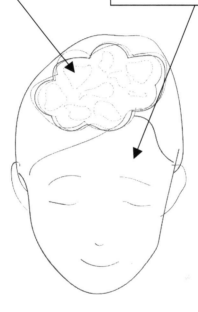

This is what you're aiming for. All the traumatic things are now within your memory only and not causing daily distress. They've always happened, but they are not in control of you anymore.

With more space, you get to deal with everyday, ordinary things in life: work, home, driving the car, making meals – all of those things that are common to everyday life. So now the previously traumatised mind has all of this space, and it takes an awful lot to fill that space up. The more space, the more there is peace within yourself, the more you heal. In turn, you get to be on the 'upward spiral' that creates more healing, and so that cycle continues.

What can you do to create headspace

✓ Re-schedule (create space in your diary)

✓ Take time off work

✓ Imagine what your life would be like if you put yourself first

✓ List what is good and not so good in your life

✓ List what or who you would like to move closer to you

✓ List what or who you would like to move further away from you

✓ Ask yourself 'do I feel nourished in my life?'

✓ List what is nourishing for you

✓ Create your 'simple list' of small things that might make a big difference (walking the dog, bathing, cooking, reading, conversation with a friend, arts and crafts, looking at maps; whatever it is)

✓ Remember to include one of the above when you're feeling full again

✓ Be kind to yourself in the time it takes to learn about creating head space

✓ Remind yourself that creating space helps you recover more quickly and be at ease more quickly too

✓ Remind yourself that this helps others around you too

Now you can feel a little bit lighter, a little bit more able to manage the everyday symptoms. This will help you continue to gain mastery over what's actually happening and what's happened to you. For a long-lasting recovery, you are aiming to live life knowing that it is healthy to create space. Space to think, feel, relax, rest, be whatever you want, to live with ease and fulfilment.

'When all your space is full, you live filled without fulfilment.'

The more you master this, the more energy and resources you have to face and process for the old things and the new things in your life. You have resilience and resources to remember experiences without distress, without crying, without being sick, without being distraught. They eventually become memories, and you create resilience; you feel strong, and you feel capable.

To be clear, I do not mean you have to process in minute detail everything that you have been through. You will find that some experiences don't even need 'looking at' because they are so similar to others. Because of how the memory networks work, you can sometimes 'mop them up' along the way.

The fact that the memory is scrambled together during 'overwhelm' (I describe it as being like a bunch of spaghetti and we are trying to take each strand at a time and decipher a way out to feeling better), it somewhat helps the brain make free associations, and if you like 'free healing.'

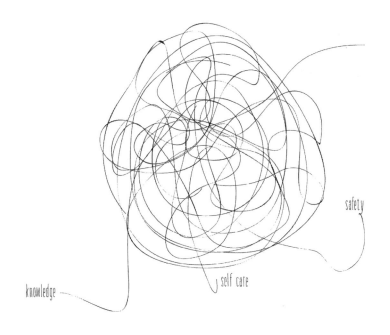

knowledge

self care

safety

As in the 'spaghetti of chaos.' Out of the chaos, it's important to find the strands that need to be attended to. It doesn't have to be everything at once or everything at all.

This is particularly useful if you are worried that you will have to dredge every single thing you've ever experienced out of the depths of your memory. In fact, recovery doesn't have to be anything like that. With the memory being all mixed up, you can deal with different things that have happened just because they are similar to

161

what you're already working on. So the reason I use the head picture is firstly, to enable you to understand what's happening to you when you are too traumatised to understand verbal language alone. And secondly, to help as a guide to what there might be for you to work on. You will find that creating your own 'head picture' in the weeks and months ahead will help you keep track of your experience and progress.

I like the analogy of the strands of spaghetti (as above) when trying to discover the important strands that are causing consistent distress. Truthfully, there tend to be only a few strands that are causing deep pain, and once these can be seen one by one, they lose some of their power immediately. Taking one strand at a time gives you some space and some solid concrete things to work on when it can be overwhelmingly difficult when the spaghetti is rolled up together. Sometimes you may find a strand and see it for what it's worth; it can seem that it needs not much particular attention at all. As you un-jumble the spaghetti, you'll experience being able to master the out-of-control 'overwhelm'. In time, you will get the much-needed feedback that recovery is not only hopeful but achievable.

Example: When there's been a build-up of stresses, a person generally has known for a really long time that they've been living out of kilter. They might be the kind of person who survives on 10 cups of coffee, 40 cigarettes, and sweet food throughout the day (if any food at all), and there's just a slow demise, but actually, it's never experienced as a slow demise, it's always experienced as a traumatic breakdown. Suddenly they can't get up in the morning; they might have a heart attack or anxiety attack or something sudden happens to them where they might be made redundant; some staff member has accused them of something, and all of a sudden, all of that stress teams up from over a decade or more, as though it's happened today, and that's what causes the overload. Those people are generally the people who are not very used to caring for themselves. They're very good at getting the job done and looking after others, but frequently there's something in their own self-care that suffers.

This chapter really, was to outline some of the things you might be going through; although every individual is different, I must stress that. Every single 'symptom landscape' for an individual is different, but I do want you to truly realise that all traumatic breakdowns have a similarity with everyone, and that is to reiterate that trauma is completely and utterly overwhelming. If it isn't, then it isn't trauma. It's nothing about you as a person; it's about the nature of the event or set of events and the consequent physiological, psychological, and emotional changes. There is a complete devastation of all senses, resources, resiliencies, somebody's ability to dig deep and pull themselves through. It's very hard to reach out for help when you feel this ghastly, but there really is hope. There is hope within the seven processes inside this book. Your road to recovery starts with being able to get safe, believing you are safe so that you can do the 'emotional work' you need to do to have a full and long-lasting recovery.

Chapter summary

Getting your head around overload; how burnout and breakdown makes you full up

How creating head space beats stress

Commit to creating head space as a way of steadying your path through recovery

Calming yourself in the turmoil is a great first step.

It's neurological, not personal.

You will recover.

Process 2:
SAFETY – STRESS hates safety – slow down and find your 'soft place to fall'

This chapter is all about safety. It's about finding an external place of safety and an internal sense of safety, because, during a traumatic breakdown, the brain has absolutely no idea that it's not within the trauma still, so you feel unsafe all the time.

How to find yourself your 'place of safety,' your 'soft place to fall.' Finding a room in the house, for instance, where you feel the safest. Be around people that you feel are the safest (this means choosing not to be around people who are not good for you) because you can't do the rest of the work you need to do to recover unless you've got this as a foundation. You can't work on your grief, your anger, your revenge fantasies, or just about anything until you feel safe to do so.

'I know you're not going to believe me that you are safe because your brain is telling you that you are not. I know it doesn't feel over either. For some of you it will feel like just the beginning. It's a case of convincing your brain

that you are safe now and in recovery. Let's get you to feel somewhat safer than you do.'

I want you to treat this like it's a project, like this is part of your work. You, your friends, your family, get a plan together of how to help your brain believe you're safe. Sometimes it can be seen as a bit of fun. You might be thinking 'How very odd to suggest this when I don't feel safe at all.' If it makes it easier for you, then imagine that it's like taking a medicine, and I'm telling you this medicine is for your road to recovery; this medicine helps. Trying to help your brain believe you're safe is an enormous step in your recovery journey.

It's a funny experience, this, because you're overwhelmed, and it seems a little bit nonsense, but the first thing is I want you to literally say out loud, **'I'm safe.'** You might need to do this twenty times a day. It might be that you have a panic attack or a sudden bout of anxiety. You might have sweats, retching, be sick and dizzy. It's never a bad thing for you to say out loud, 'I'm safe – it's okay; it's over.' Just so that at some level, your mind and your body gets some feedback other than fear alone. Eventually, the mind and the body start to believe it and to take it on board.

The other thing you can do is literally make a safe place. It might be your bedroom, living room, office. You might say it has flowers in it; you might say it has the bedding you love in it. I actually am a big believer in using a bedroom as a safe place (if indeed it can be) when you feel least safe, are threatened and very afraid; actually just to go to bed for a short while because whilst your whole body is experiencing being on a soft mattress with a duvet around you with your head on the pillow, you might feel absolutely wretched, but the body, at many levels, is getting some feedback that you are safe (its fancy name is proprioception). Even if you've got such a terror inside about whatever is happening or happened, the feedback neurologically is that you're safe in a bed. It's useful to do this for short periods. If you fear you won't get up again, put a timer on and allow yourself say a half an hour of complete bed time, so you get consistent feedback that you are not under threat and are safe.

What small thing can you have with you to help you feel safe?

It's also useful for you to draw a place of safety. You might draw a sea or a beach if that's the place where you feel the most relaxed. You might draw a rainbow, or your bedroom, your living room, your partner with whom you feel safest. With these miniature images (usually 1.5 inches square) you can discreetly carry them around in your pocket or your wallet so they can engender feelings of safety and relaxation when you least feel it.

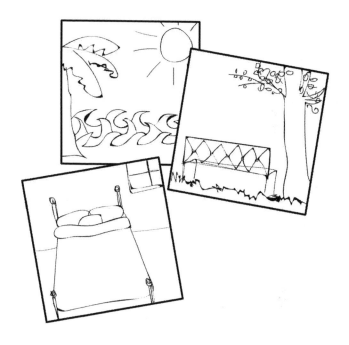

Apart from just 'tricking' the brain for a little bit out of its torment, it also can be releasing endorphins and helping calm your system down. Endorphins are one of our free natural euphoric remedies and our 'free painkiller.' When we are amidst burnout and breakdown, we experience a reduction if not cessation of endorphin production. The naturally occurring 'stress-reducing' chemicals in our body, such as dopamine, serotonin, and oxytocin are not produced as efficiently. Mood and motivation are dramatically affected; therefore, ordinary methods of raising mood/positivity are not as readily available to you. The ordinary ways to release endorphins are:

- Connecting with other people.

- What we eat (can become overeating/ comfort eating in the dependency on the immediate endorphin release).

- Exercise.

So you can see that it becomes an unbearable cycle of feeling cornered and not easily finding a way out towards the upward spiral. You can see why people may take it into their own hands to find a way to dampen down their extreme stress reaction. This is commonly known as 'self-medicating.' This can be in the form of numbing oneself psychologically, and physically; taking prescription drugs and un-prescribed drugs, alcohol, and other substances. The sudden flash of burnout and breakdown renders you unable initially to tap into these naturally occurring chemicals. It doesn't remain this way. As you increase your space to deal with every day and your hope grows, you will be increasingly able to reactivate these natural ways of healing.

Of course, sadly for some in the world, it's impossible to find safety, and so recovery will be prolonged and tormenting. In these instances, recovery will be elusive, and support will be required to keep despair at bay. Most of us in the UK are fortunate to be able to re-establish safety, physically first if not psychologically for a while.

'Breathing is your best friend'

One of the other things to use to aid your recovery is to learn what is called 'self-soothing.' This is where you learn techniques to calm yourself down. You'll find the methods that work for you. When you feel like you're going into a panic or you're reacting to the adrenalin that's flying through your system, you can do some deep breathing; some self-reassurance that you're safe.

As you practice, you can slow your breathing, and slow your pulse rate down. This will be a technique that will be part of your lifelong skillskit.

Our natural reaction in panic is to breathe faster, and as we stumble to catch another breath, we breathe faster and faster as we panic more.

Here is a simple 'mobile' breathing technique:

Focus on something literally or in your mind's eye. If you can put one hand on the bottom of your sternum and slowly breathe in for three seconds and on the fourth second breathe out. Massage or tap with your hand your sternum and this will calm you immediately. This is a little technique you can do no matter where you are. Do this for three breaths not too quickly and not too deeply as it's for calming and moving your attention to safety, and beyond anxiety. It's important that you don't become anxious in using this technique well. It allows you the moment, the sensation, and the knowledge of soothing yourself and your system.

That's one of the key skills to be able to recover and look at difficult things that you've been through. It's necessary to be able to calm yourself down, throughout your recovery journey. What I don't want is that you are terrified about what you've been through and having to recall it and that traumatises you all over again.

Useful guidance for calming

- Take as much control of your environment as possible.

- Reduce the external stimuli around you.

- Watch less television, if any at all. Maybe it's worth just not watching any television for a while unless it's films where you know what the story is. What the brain doesn't need is something in a news item that you are not aware is happening, and that is 'fed' to you unexpectedly. When you're in an emotional state of 'not being able to take anymore' that's exactly what it means. It means you need to reduce the chance of anything else happening. Unexpected news items can become what we call 'a traumatic trigger;' a traumatic trigger being anything in your external environment that produces a reaction of stress and distress. When your head is already full, reducing the chances of filling the tiny little space that you have left to deal with every day is crucial, simple but crucial (see head picture in the previous chapter). So cutting out or down on television and newspapers are generally good for a while, even if that's what you're used to; it is a good way of reducing the stimuli and/or the fear of threat. It's all part of your recovery project.

- Ask others in the family and around you to keep hold of the information. If you work in professional life, and you have been through traumatic breakdown, the last thing you need to know is what other people are thinking about it or how the news is reporting it.

- Reach out for help. Don't delay this in the hope you can do it all by yourself. You deserve to feel better quickly, and it's really tough to recover alone.

It is about achieving a place where you're not as overwhelmed as you were. These simple protective mechanisms are crucial in reducing the stress upon the already over-stressed mind and body. It is particularly useful for those looking after you to know these things and reducing your feelings of helplessness.

One common feature you might find in yourself is your need to tell your story (even if you've forgotten what you have said and who you have told, due to short-term memory loss). Of course, you need to be considerate of who you tell your story to. By all means, tell your story as much as you want to if you feel you can trust who you are telling. It's really important for you to be able to tell your story and not be silenced.

The other thing that gives you an outlet for your story is to write it. If you write in freehand, research suggests that that's very healing. So you might write pages and pages and pages of your story, how you feel, what you feel angry about, what you might do in the future, what you might never do, what you regret. It doesn't matter as long as you're writing it down freehand and keeping that safe somewhere in a notebook.

Another useful tip is to doodle. You don't have to be good at drawing, but there's something very relaxing to the brain if we doodle slowly. If we doodle fast, that actually tends to be over-stimulating. It's just a little bit of doodling, and the reason I call it 'doodling' is because I want to encourage you to do it but not think you've got to be good at art.

Six simple tasks to feeling better in the moment

1. **Telling yourself this is an ordinary reaction to an extraordinary situation helps A LOT.** It reminds you that you're not losing your mind; it reminds you that you are facing extraordinary circumstances, and your body and mind are reacting as they should. That doesn't mean it's okay by you; it just means its normal, so you don't have to worry anymore about the reasons.

2. **Talking to people who you can trust about your experience helps**. Years ago, we would talk things through again and again with our extended families. Now we must find a 'listening ear,' someone who is prepared to listen to your story over and over again.

3. **Writing down your thoughts and feelings help.** It is proven that writing freehand reduces emotional agony. You need never look back at what you write (you might just

put it away somewhere), but writing is a healer.

4. **Doodling helps.** Making pictures has a similar effect as writing. It can be an expression of how you feel inside or an image which simply acts as a distraction. (It doesn't need to be a piece of art; doodling slowly helps calm the mind and body).

5. **Going for a walk helps.** If this is available to you, this is a good way of reducing emotional agony. It can help calm stress and simply gives a distraction whilst taking in the surroundings. Walking gives positive physical feedback to the brain and body. If a walk outside is not possible, even around the garden will do, or opening a door or window to take in some fresh air will help!

6. **Speaking kindly to yourself helps.** It has been proven that how we think influences how we feel. So, when you say kind things even in your own mind, your subconscious hears, and you begin to believe it. The reverse is the same! So whilst you're in any kind of distress today, try speaking kindly to yourself. All inner brutality of thought creates

more suffering. Be kindly and companionable to yourself always. Try this: 'It's a shame I feel this way; it won't last.'

What can people do to help?

I think the role of other people is crucial in reducing your isolation. If you feel alienated and devastated, the last thing you want to experience is people turning their back on you. The majority of us are wired to connect with others, so to be 'disconnected' at your most vulnerable isn't helpful. It's still not helpful even when we think we are glad of people not seeing us at our worst. Isolation is not your 'friend' during this time, even if the humiliation and shame you feels 'tells' you it's easier to hide. It may help for short periods, but prolonged time alone when you cannot rely on yourself for positive feedback and reassurance can prolong your recovery. If you feel you have few genuine friends around you, consider getting professional support in the form of counselling, psychotherapy, or therapeutic coaching, for example. This can decrease your symptoms and raise your confidence, and just so that you know, any genuinely good professional will understand what it has taken for you to take that step.

People can help by picking up the phone and by telling you about the 'day-to-day,' but just asking how you are and telling you how their day was, or even by popping around, making a cup of tea, just doing some normal things. As I said before, helping by the simplest of gestures, 'I'll come around and I'll watch a film with you,' that kind of thing is all the body and mind needs. Some normality.

People can also help you feel safe by reducing the amount of news, gossip, and public news that is brought into your life. For example, they can be very considerate of the types of material you can be exposed to and that you 'can tolerate.' It won't always be the case that you will need protecting, but certainly in the early days of being completely overwhelmed, you'll struggle to cope with any more stimuli. It's imperative that you are not triggered into flashbacks or flashbulb memories. It also helps to reduce the 'shots' of stress hormones and encourages the upward spiral of mastering traumatic burnout and breakdown.

So, in the early days, you are looking to create an environment where your whole system (mind and body) can recover enough to be able to work through what's happening to you. As time goes by, you slowly but surely make space for everyday bigger and bigger and last for longer. This provides a place for hope to grow and healing to start.

People around you can gently remind you of how to take small steps in self-care and in safety measures as above. You will feel incredibly vulnerable and thrown back to feeling very young again, requiring some looking after. People can help you with this feeling of being 'thrown backwards' by helping you understand that it won't last.

If you can't easily get to a place where you feel there is safety and hope of recovery on your own and with friends and family, you can reach out for professional guidance and support. Finding someone to help you decipher the information either by reading or consulting professionals including GPs helps you navigate the passage of recovery. Reaching out to others and asking for even the smallest gestures of support will help you. People close to you generally want to help, especially when they care for you and love you.

So, to summarize this chapter, we've covered why finding a place where you start to feel safe is very important; we've talked about making this your first step on the road to recovery; we've talked about how people can help themselves, and we've talked about how others can help too. This has also been summarised into six secrets to feeling safe as above.

Chapter summary

Asking people NOT to tell you what's in the news.

DON'T watch television for a while.

Watch a film where you know what the beginning, middle, and ending are going to be.

Breathe through your worst anxiety episodes.

Write your story down.

Write your feelings down.

Doodle in a notebook.

Find professional help. If you have a hunch you need it, you're probably right. The quicker you get the support, the better for you.

Feeling safe, even though you don't at the moment, is the first part of your journey. The second part of your journey is learning how to look after yourself when you feel least like doing so.

Process 3:
CARE ABOUT YOU – STRESS THRIVES ON YOU HATING YOURSELF – beat it with love and kindness

This chapter is all about self-care: how to look after yourself when you feel so dreadful you feel you can't or don't want to. One of the most common reactions to turmoil is you stop being able to or desiring to look after yourself.

The experience of being shunted into an agonizing world of anxiety, depression, fear, neurological symptoms may have prompted you to turn against yourself. Maybe you've never fully cared about yourself. You might be feeling that you have brought this upon yourself, and now you're angry with yourself for breaking down and not being able to shake it off. As I'm writing this book, it seems that I'm describing what would be obvious to most, but I just want to be clear that actually we don't live in a culture of supporting people in turmoil. Even today, we still feel that something as unpleasant as trauma, burnout or breakdown is contagious. People naturally tend to want to stay away from despair, so I just want to be clear that it's really significant when people turn away. We were talking about hyper-vigilance in the chapter on Knowledge; this very symptom makes people in burnout and breakdown particularly vigilant about and sensitive to being deserted. It's not unlike bereaved people noticing people crossing the street or saying 'you find out who your friends are.' And it's often not that they're not our friends; it is simply because it's so incredibly uncomfortable to be near people who are literally in physical, psychological, and emotional disarray that they just can't find it in themselves to be close.

When you are traumatised and taken out of the life you knew and with all your confusing and agonizing 'spaghetti of symptoms,' you will find you lose the ability (for a while) to do or care about the straightforward tasks. Fully and previously highly functioning people are thrown into a place of struggling to eat; to shower; to sleep; to dress; to work; to care. These are common reactions to 'the overwhelm', and as I previously stated, it's very helpful for you to be around those who really care when you feel you cannot.

So this chapter is all about the tiny steps you can take to looking after yourself, and how these tiny steps can lead to massive leaps and gains.

How do you start looking after yourself? – Companionship (solidarity with yourself)

The first and most important decision for you to make in your self-care plan is to find compassion for what you've been through. I like to call it companionship. Create a companionable relationship with yourself, not a mean, demeaning and angry relationship with yourself. You will not recover fully whilst you continue to hurt yourself as a result of what you've been through already. I can absolutely guarantee you that you will not recover as long as you hurt yourself further. That's a given, basically, so it really has to start there. Forgive yourself for whatever you are berating yourself about; for example, not seeing the trauma coming, not being able to run from the danger, for speeding and feeling like you've caused the accident. People really don't intend to bring trauma upon themselves; otherwise, it's not trauma. You didn't set out to be shocked by burnout and breakdown, and accepting this early on will set you free. Feel some compassion for what you've been through, and enable yourself to continue the journey towards full recovery. You may berate yourself for what you've been through in a way to take some control over an event that was out of your control in the first place. You may talk to yourself cruelly in an attempt not to have to feel the weight of the loss, grief and sadness you feel. In other words, making an attempt to be on top of the upward spiral but not truly being there.

This lack of compassion for yourself is entirely understandable; rarely do we feel prepared to face agonising feelings. It tends to make sense to us to do our damnedest to avoid them. I've no judgement about this at all; I just feel that if you allow those difficult feelings, you move through them more quickly. Who has ever woken up and decided 'I think I'll have a dose of grief today please?' So, lack of compassion makes sense, but compassion for what you're going through is your golden ticket. If you are consistently companionable to yourself throughout your recovery, it simply doesn't hurt as much.

It is completely natural to experience grief if you lost something that you loved and cared about, even if that means your own physical and mental health. Grief is a normal reaction to loss which often means having to 'cry buckets of tears.' If you don't cry them, you carry them around as a weight to bear, and you're risking the tears slopping out all over the place and impinging on your day to day life now and in your future. Allowing your grief and other people permitting your grief and supporting you with it allows your authentic experience, and you then are more able to enter the other processes of recovery.

What might you be doing right now that's not helping?

Of course, by the time you're reading this, you have already had perhaps weeks, months even years of agonising turmoil. You'll now recognise whether you are metaphorically hitting yourself round the head with a big stick. Lack compassion for yourself for what you've been through and are going through means you often hurt yourself further, and you turn your anger against yourself. You may feel frustration and the injustice of your predicament. This creates despair, despondency, or self-loathing.

Example: People who are stripped out of their

working lives and find themselves stuck at home often judge themselves harshly, literally smacking themselves in the face or shouting at themselves, feeling less of a person now they cannot 'perform' the way they are used to.

Of course, one of the first things that is useful to know is that you've acknowledged and reached out for help. Permitting yourself to vulnerability is, in fact, a tremendous strength, and it will certainly serve to aid your recovery. I understand that this may well be irksome at best and terrifying at worst as you are not used to being the one needing the help. Here's an early key to making this easier for you, though. Allow yourself to be supported, and you will be through this quicker. You will learn about yourself quicker, and you will learn about what others need, and both will last you for life. I have immense respect for people getting to that point as I've got a fairly good idea of what it's taken from them to do that. And I'm not just meaning that in words; I'm meaning that to truly understand what it's taken from someone who has never asked for help or is the one that helps others; is the pillar of the community; is the employer of thousands of people getting to the point where they are the one that needs to reach out to help is a monumental decision requiring considerable courage.

Low-level scorn towards yourself has an insidious effect on your self-esteem. Even if you are not physically hurting yourself, berating yourself for what you have been through maintains the levels of pain and simply means you have this to overcome as well as your burnout and breakdown in the first place. Imagine you doing this to someone you loved. They have just had the hardest time in their lives, and you can see it will take them a while to recover. Would you shout at them, curse them, and be-little them? For most, I doubt you would. You would know that that would not help them at all, and it would

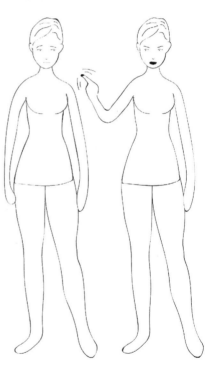

make them feel worse; it will prolong their recovery period, and it will hurt them. You have, however, by accident permitted yourself to do all of those things to yourself.

What's fabulous to know is that the use of companionship for yourself does the exact opposite. It will speed up your recovery; it will help you feel valued and better, and it is comforting. All the ingredients you need to continue your healing journey.

How would it be if the scorn was dropped, and you become the person who cares the most for what you've been through? You're now the person who when you feel low, you offer yourself a cup of tea; you don't shout at yourself, or hurt yourself. You offer encouragement and comfort. You speak softly and with support for when this recovery journey gets tough again. You remind yourself that you've had tough times before, and they won't last. It won't be long before the upward spiral becomes obvious again.

What a completely different environment within which to recover. It's an environment with an atmosphere of respect and tenderness that gives you the best foundation for dealing with this arduous journey.

Example: People tend to berate themselves, taunt themselves into feeling badly about what's happened, feeling that they made the wrong decisions, and that's what made it happen. I often ask them to visualise how big the stick is that they 'hit' themselves with. This is 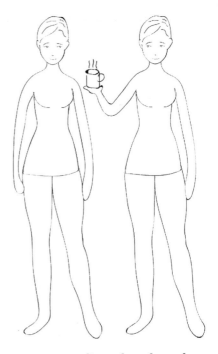 partly so that they can externalise the thought process that becomes stronger the longer it stays within a person, like a secret punishment, or torture. When it is visualised it looks less; it can't easily exist outside the person's head. Whether it's like a thin stick or a broomstick or a tree trunk, once it's outside of us, we have a better chance of mastering it, and better still, stopping it. It's already bad enough; how interesting that we find more ways to increase the pain. Somebody did say that theirs was so big they couldn't pick it up, which was quite interesting because if they couldn't pick it up, then they couldn't really hurt themselves with it. This made us laugh. Imagine for yourself the size of the stick you berate and hit yourself with. I worked with a woman one time that chose the branch of a tree and dragged it from the woods so that I could see it. Not only too big to pick up but twice the size of her; now that is a big hill to climb to recovery. This was a great metaphor for being in something that feels bigger than you as a person, and that the level of self-hatred was bigger than you too.

So, the first thing then, in summary, is supporting people to understand that, yes, it's a natural reaction to lack compassion for yourself, but it's really okay to feel a little bit sorry for what you've been through too. We tend to have such a problem with self-pitying in this world that we actually go to the other extreme and carry on regardless.

Carrying on without regard is stripping life down to a raw bare minimum of experience.' Carry on regardless,' meaning carry on without regard to yourself or anyone, is such a harsh but pervasive culture we live in. You'll notice how people talk about what's happened to them, and there's always a 'But I shouldn't have been there,' or, 'I should have been able to see that coming.' 'No point being upset, must carry on regardless.' Relinquishing the big stick and putting it in its place is a truly essential step. Ask yourself how it helps you to punish yourself further. You might be unable to see it at first, but as I said before, it could be that deep down it saves you from grief, from grieving.

Simple self-care steps make a tricky journey possible. It's not easy for us to forgive ourselves when it's affected our lives so badly. The big stick is really attached to feeling ashamed. Shame, as I have previously said, is a normal emotion to regret or embarrassment, but overwhelming shame does nothing apart from hurt us; it doesn't hurt anybody else, in reality. The feelings remain in the confines of your own mind and body, and in there it keeps you imprisoned. It does a great job of keeping you small, hidden, and paralysed.

It might help keep you in your place. If you've been assaulted, raped or have had another type of personal attack on you, the only person that benefits from your shame is the perpetrator. They're quite happy that you've become small and silent, unwell for the moment and stuck. For you trying to recover, that doesn't help you at all. I don't want you to feel ashamed for feeling ashamed either. It's about helping you understand and bring that into your conscious. That it's not okay what you went through, and seek some support if you need it.

The next thing you might struggle with looking after yourself is you might not be able to eat. You don't eat at all, or you don't eat well. So nutritionally, you start to suffer as well. That also means that your body and mind don't have the nutrition to deal with the recovery. Lack of nutrition will compound the symptoms too. That's something you can pick off in small chunks – excuse the pun, but just bit by bit, bite by bite helping you feel able to eat a little bit of healthy food and drinking water, at least. Occasionally after the initial days following the shock, some may eat too much to deal with the emotional agony, but it tends to start with not eating, to begin with.

Getting some control when everything else is out of control

A common symptom of extreme stress is lack of appetite. This can be due to physiological changes: the dysregulation experienced including the myriad of chemicals zooming around your body. This can also be exacerbated by the difficulty in self-care in the early stages of breakdown. This means that you may struggle to eat well because of how dreadful you feel emotionally. And once again, this becomes one of those difficult cycles within which you can find yourself. Not being able to eat healthy and nutritious food means that your body whilst going through its greatest stress has the poorest quality of nutrition to sustain it. This is entirely to be expected initially. If you can steadily introduce regular sips of water, healthy snacks whether that is fruit or nuts on as a regular basis as you can tolerate. As I have said many times before, the early stages of burnout and breakdown are all about finding your first step forward to recovery; this will come quicker with the best nutrition you can stomach. So, even when you don't feel hungry or thirsty, tiny nutritional snacks will help give your whole system feedback that you are taking the best care even when you least feel like doing so and least feel able. Slowly but surely, this engenders the upward spiral. You begin to feel you gain some control over things that used to be unconscious. This means you pull back some of your mastery over this extraordinarily difficult experience. As you make these seemingly tiny steps, you will be moving up the spiral so that you stand on top of your experience, and your experience doesn't stand and trample all over you.

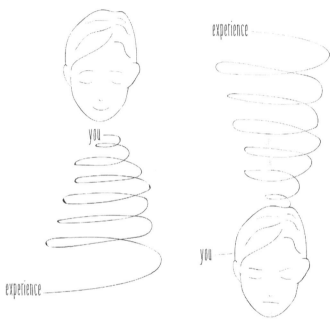

Spiral upwards and spiral downwards. It's a spiral because it is a journey, and it's gently sloping rather than sudden gains (though these are not impossible). It's slippery so that you can also find yourself going downwards

and upwards, but working consistently towards being on top of your experience and not the other way round.

The other very common not-looking-after-yourself symptom is what generally, in the psychotherapy field is called self-medicating, which can be alcohol, drugs, food, or distracting behaviours like gambling. The thing about this is it's a double-edged sword because people tend to think that they are actually looking after themselves because they can't feel the pain. So it does have a sense of 'care' about it. By the time you've had three pints of beer, or three glasses of wine, the agony that you were in has somewhat diminished, so it is a crude way of looking after yourself to begin with. The problem is when this tips over to being dependency and addiction. The important element to this is for you to understand that's why you are drinking so much and are medicating the symptoms. It's perfectly natural to want to remove yourself from the agony. The problem then is that the psychological injury is actually still there. As stated previously, I'm a big believer in the environment for recovery having to be without judgement, but with noticing and companionship with yourself. In my experience, most people generally embark on over-consumption of alcohol and self-medication in the early stages to manage the intolerable and deaden the unendurable until such a time that the fog of the storm recedes, and/or someone reaches for help. The issue I feel that is worth addressing here is that you do the best you can not to stack up entrenched behaviours or health problems that will require further attention in your future. You have an opportunity now to recover, heal, and move on.

The other thing that doesn't help you in post-burnout and breakdown is when you isolate yourself. Some quiet and time alone are essential if they aren't prolonged. You may want to hide away due to shame. It may be you simply feel fear of exposure or feeling very vulnerable. Time away from other people is a good thing if it's nourishing, if it gives you strength to continue your recovery. Long periods of hiding away can cause agoraphobic symptoms, however, so it may help to gently challenge yourself to stay connected with other people.

You might struggle to reach out for help; perhaps you're not the type that reaches out for help easily. Go back to treating it as a project. You'd get help for a project house or a work project; you'd seek the right type of advice or guidance, and you'd seek to fill the gaps in your knowledge and skills. Treat this the same and speed up feeling better.

The other thing you'll find works to begin with but doesn't aid your recovery, is suppressing your emotional life in order to stay in control of feelings and symptoms. This is initially useful to dampen down your feelings, but a long-term suppression of feelings leads to depression so that we then have a breakdown and depression to deal with as well. Remember everything you deal with now will be one less thing you have to deal with in your future. If reaching out for help feels hard, at least remind yourself that by attending now and working with it, you've taken steps to look after yourself and invest in your long-term recovery.

Can you recover if you don't look after yourself?

If you don't make attempts to look after yourself, you won't be able to go through the processes in their most valuable order. That doesn't mean to say there's an A to Z of recovery, but I do believe there are processes, like I said earlier. If you don't become companionable to yourself and treat yourself with kindness, consideration, and care, you continue to hurt yourself, and you have less chance of fully recovering. You might find your symptoms become easier in the course of time, but if you don't feel sorry for what you've been through and had to face (and that's not wallowing in self-pity, that's taking responsibility for how you feel), you just simply can't make the next part of the process thoroughly. So, this can then lead to suppression of symptoms that will lead to depression and often anxiety as well. Some kind of recovery will happen. It'll be like the scar tissue becomes healed over but healed to leave a scar that's visible, and it will then impinge and encroach on your life. For instance, somebody that suppresses and doesn't work through the trauma may never work again.

Example: They may never face being at work, in an office, never act again, never write, never create, or be vulnerable ever again. They may never face being in a boardroom, or drive a car or use public transport. This is a common aftermath in people after breakdown.

If this is the case for you, then professional help will be your quickest way of feeling better. There are so many ways to help your whole system recover and to de-sensitise what your system believes to be the threat. Check out the list of available support at the back of this book.

Another way to help yourself desensitise difficult situations is to practice in tiny chunks your ability to cope with the situation. It can aid recovery substantially and quickly by simply practising these things.

Example: Somebody has difficulty driving the car; they might need to practice being the passenger of the car to begin with. It might also be useful for them to sit in the driver's seat without driving.

There are many different ways of approaching and desensitising the stuff you find trickiest and the stuff you need to do day-to-day to make your life whole. This is something that needs consideration, and to be done at your own pace. It is vital that exposing yourself to this does not worsen your symptoms: the distress will hinder your recovery and frighten your whole system again if done without consideration. I find it extremely helpful to explore 'frame by frame' the things that are a struggle to approach. If, for example, you need to approach talking in front of 300 people which would be ordinary and in your everyday life, you can draw out frame by frame on paper the scenario with its beginning, middle, and end. Using this technique will help you discover what part you are truly avoiding. For example, the drawings may illuminate that the fear is about what people think. The drawings may illuminate that the fear is about being attacked again. Invariably, a lot of the fears are about appearing vulnerable and weak. This viewing can help decipher what is the fear and the bit that keeps you stuck. If you know what it is, you have a better chance of overcoming it. Like the upward spiral, you become the master of your experience, not the other way round. It might appear a cruel twist to you that as someone who has already been traumatised you now have to work through the process to full recovery. You may experience this as an enormous injustice. It's easy to see how that would be the case. It's truly worth allowing this anger, this appropriate anger, in order to release you to a place where you can start making steps to recovery and having the best life you can have.

Let's go back to shame briefly

Why do you feel ashamed?

You may feel that you shouldn't react this way.

You should know better, and something shouldn't take you off your feet to this magnitude.

You feel you should be able to get yourself better, and you feel weak if you haven't.

Any element of public humiliation makes all this worse.

Perhaps you are the fixers; the doers; the helpers; the business builders; the case builders; the 'well-known' for your strengths.

When you become the victim, of course you are weakened, and you are vulnerable at this time.

The thing about shame, if it becomes overwhelming, is that it becomes crippling and causes inertia. It causes a type of paralysis because while shame is left and you don't put compassion and companionability in its place, it just grows and grows. It becomes overwhelming and insurmountable, and shame is nearly always associated with some kind of public humiliation; from wetting yourself in front of classmates to misdemeanours in the House of Commons. The public element to anything, if it isn't the celebration of you, always has the capability to humiliate you, expose you and your vulnerability. If you work with people who have had a media campaign against them, for instance, and they've lived and worked in the public eye, they often will say at least when something bad happens to others, at least it happens in private.

What I tend to say to people is to start at least wrestling with the feelings of shame because we can't just eradicate them just because I say it's not useful; it's finding out where it has its 'footholds,' where it has its strength, and if it's related to anything else that's happened in your life. What I say to you is, start trying to say 'What a shame that happened,' not 'Shame on you.' We tend to say, 'Shame on me that that happened,' or 'I made that happen,' instead of 'What a shame that happened.' It seems like a really simple and trite way of wrestling with something so over-whelming, but it does work.

When you allow yourself this, you really will understand that is a very different way of looking at it. I'm asking you just to practice it. Practice saying it, and then you might start believing it. The other thing you might say is 'How does shame serve me? How does it work for me?' Part of me wants to say, 'Look, drop it, it doesn't work,' but it's finding out why it does work in some way and if it helps you. Usually, it doesn't, but we are a nation confusing looking after ourselves with self-pity, so we think that if we don't feel ashamed, we're going to wallow and eventually drown in our self-pity. That simply is so far from the truth, that we are immobilising people.

One of the things that I've been paying attention to over the last few years is looking at how shame works and how it resides in the body. My belief is that there's a direct correlation between the amount of shame and intensity of shame and the energy this requires. If you propel that energy in the opposite direction on purpose, i.e. , transform the energy it takes to maintain shame then you get to use it as positive energy in the healing and reconstruction of your life. Overwhelming shame and horror keeps you still, paralyses your recovery. If you can find the energy behind that and re-direct that upon your path of recovery, it becomes part of your personal power and positive energy to propel you into the healing process. I'm not saying that's easy. It's one of the most difficult things to treat and stand up to because by the time it's obvious what's in the way, it is beautifully constructed, and so robust that it feels like it's part of you forever. It feels insurmountable, but it is not.

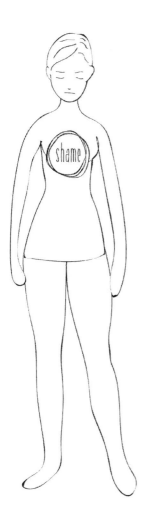

Shame and other feelings we don't attend to reside within us, and are easily hidden at first.

We walk around with them and no one knows they are there.

We believe they are part of us forever, and they are who we are as people because we have 'swallowed' the feelings for so long we don't realise they are just feelings and not part of our character.

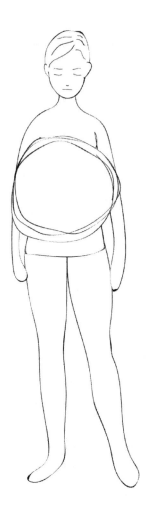

Unattended shame and other suppressed feelings grow within us. They will start to affect the decisions we make, but we may well not be aware of it.

We will be avoiding things and people in order not to provoke this feeling within us, which is growing without us knowing.

We might have a sense that something is different about us but it doesn't have a name; it's weighty and unformed.

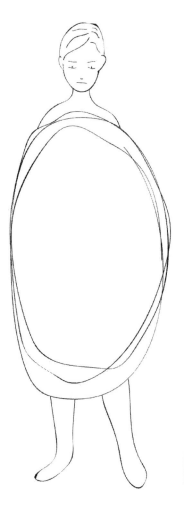

We come to have an increasing sense of something growing within us, that doesn't make us feel good.

It becomes heavy and we are aware we're carrying something around, and it's in the way.

We don't know what it is and we can't name it.

We can't easily embrace all the things we want to do in life and can't harness our potential. Things start feeling difficult to manage.

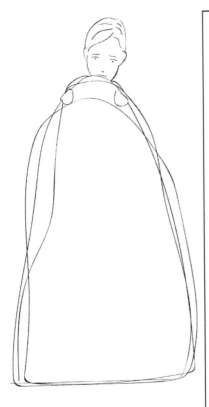

Eventually, shame becomes big enough to obscure your vision.

It keeps you hidden away, feeling small and overwhelmed.

You know there is something in the way, but you're not entirely sure which emotion it is. The most common growing emotions that hide us and become overwhelmingly heavy are shame, grief, and anger.

At least now we know that something is big and in the way, this is our best chance of overcoming it.

What will help you look after yourself?

Going back again to compassion, reiterating 'What a shame that happened' or 'It's a shame that happened to me,' really allowing yourself to be the victim of something so that you can move through it. My feeling is that for optimum performance, you require optimum companionship with yourself. If you don't start with compassion for yourself, you'll never really get to optimum performance, because you'll be expending energy, suppressing symptoms, feeling bad about yourself, feeling shame which is using energy every single day. You will massively delay your recovery if you cannot be companionable to yourself. Another way of looking at it is looking at the analogy of the wall of water. If you imagine a wall of water, or if you dive into a swimming pool and you don't get it right, it really hurts. If you smack water, it actually hurts. If you hit a wall of water, it hurts, but if you decide you're going to swim through it, it doesn't hurt so much. Swim with the 'tide of recovery,' and it will simply be easier.

As depicted by the image below: recovery from burnout and breakdown if you decide to 'swim' with the process is not going to be easy, but it won't hurt as much as punching it and smacking your head against it.

If you keep hitting the wall of water, it will remain and hurt, but if you decide one day to swim through the wall of water, it's a much easier journey to get to the other side and doesn't hurt half as much.

Throw away the big stick

If you manage to embrace compassion for yourself and become companionable towards what you've been through, you will naturally have thrown your big stick away. It can feel such a familiar big stick, and if you feel like picking it up again, just ask yourself how it's going to help you.

Using the idea of companionship for yourself for what you've been through will help 'minimise the size of the stick' and eventually eradicate it. When you finally put the big stick down, you will find your recovery accelerates dramatically.

Eat and drink well

Eating and drinking as well as you can manage is all part of your self-care plan. Even if this means having the tiniest amount of food every hour, you will find it helps you feel like you're doing something to put yourself on the mend. Regular sips of water to keep you hydrated is very important. Morsels of nutritious food that don't overwhelm you but give you the vitamins and minerals you need is very important. Taking some advice from a nutritional expert can help too. Look at reputable online health food stores for vitamin and mineral supplements. These initial steps back to healthy eating will give your body and mind the best chance to withstand the rigours of the symptom onslaught of burnout and breakdown talked about in the chapter about Knowledge.

Be conscious of self-medicating

Become conscious, and purposefully notice what you are doing in order to dampen down the tumultuous emotions and thoughts that are zooming around your body and mind. It can be invaluable for you to talk this over with a doctor, to discuss at length whether a course of prescribed medication would suit you. Medication in the short term can be necessary and helpful in the early stages of traumatic breakdown. Having a GP, naturopath, homeopath, kinesiologist, for example, support you and monitor your needs is often crucial in order to establish feeling able to function on a day-to-day basis. Many people are understandably afraid to take the support of medication, but it is a much more refined industry these days, and the priority in the early stages is to get yourself feeling calmer and safer. We often turn to readily available medications like alcohol, drugs, and caffeine which often can consequently give us another predicament to overcome.

Therapeutic work to help you overcome burnout, breakdown, stress, or traumatic experience can be done to some extent alongside prescribed medication. It is, however, phenomenally difficult if not impossible to enter into therapeutic work when self-medicating (i.e. under the influence).

It is a perfectly natural response to want and need to dampen overwhelming sensations within the mind and body. It does, however, often cause tremendous feelings of guilt, shame, and embarrassment, and so once again we come full circle to the steps required to recover. Feeling sorry for what you've been through and being companionable to yourself for the steps that you've taken to manage your overwhelming symptoms without judgement is essential. I cannot do justice to this subject in this book, but there are many specialist resources that can help you if you feel your self-medicating is controlling you (becoming habit and addiction); some of these will be at the end of the book.

Get rest if not sleep

It can be incredibly difficult to relax and to settle the mind enough to sleep. Try not to hold this against yourself, and try not to worry (I know that's easier said than done). Obviously, sleep is a crucial element to being able to have respite and to restore our energy and resources. It can become a cruel, vicious circle when overwhelmed; when we need sleep more than ever, it eludes us. Finding ways to get rest if not sleep is an important part of self-care. Things like taking a bath with lavender oil (natural relaxant), and clary sage oil (natural anti-depressant), going to bed for power naps, listening to music or listening to audio books in order to provide some respite.

It is sometimes those simple attempts to rest and not to force sleep upon us that make the difference. You do eventually start to sleep properly again. The greatest support to you when you are in the tricky times of not being able to sleep is to know that it won't last. Once you can read again, you can purposefully take rest times and catch up on reading you intended to door have wanted to do. As it all gets easier and you're on the upward spiral, you will be able to watch old films, new films, even terrestrial television again!

Basically, the best remedy to not being able to sleep is to try not to worry about it. Know it gets better. If you struggle to sleep for months on end, do speak to your GP; they can sometimes support you with short courses of medication that will 'interrupt' the non-sleeping pattern.

Have compassion for yourself, which probably comes first, and then you feel like you can at least look after yourself and eat better and get some sleep. If we don't make these initial steps, it will prolong recovery. It doesn't make it impossible; it just makes it take longer. What we're looking for, I would say, is an upward spiral. When we catch ourselves hurting ourselves or not looking after ourselves, we give ourselves a little bit more to recover from. Again, what I would say is to use this as information to say, 'Okay, I hurt myself with that,' or 'I'm feeling bad that this happened,' so that you can go in an upward spiral to full recovery. It is the normal course of things for you to feel frightened, frustrated, and worried about your recovery. Speaking to yourself without cruel judgements and punitive overtone can help you feel hope. Instead of judging yourself, make a judgement about your situation instead. Judging yourself and making a judgement is different. Later on, I talk about the power of noticing something in this context means to take a look at it in a sense without judgement. To notice without judgement means gathering information that can help you with your journey. This is a powerful way to maintain your recovery when we cannot see the 'wood for the trees' or 'the healing amongst the agony.'

The other thing is, just about everybody that's ever been through a burnout and breakdown will come to the point where they can't do this alone, and every single person needs a leg up in life. It's almost impossible to do this alone because our ability to decipher our path out of the complexity of post-burnout and breakdown is hindered if not obliterated.

Chapter summary

Things to remember about love and kindness to you:

Work towards having a companionable relationship with yourself. Where you treat yourself with love and kindness even if you don't like everything you are or what you've been through.

Feel sorry for what you've been through; don't worry about self-pity it's very unlikely!

Throw away the big stick, if you haven't already.

Eat and drink as well as you can manage. Good nutrition fuels the body & mind.

Take a shower; put on make-up; have a shave.

Be conscious of self-medicating; seek support if necessary.

Get rest if not sleep, and try not to worry, sleepless nights won't last.

Draw and write.

Get the help you deserve for a speedy recovery; don't suffer longer than you need.

Remember you will recover.

Process 4:
HELP – your antidote to stress – allow help from professionals, friends, and family

If you've struggled to function for more than a month, get professional guidance as to what to do next. There are plenty of well-qualified helpers out there.

Let's explode the myth around needing help right away. I can guarantee all readers of this book that every single human that has ever lived and lives now needs a helping hand now and again. That can be someone holding a ladder for them, looking after their children or their elderly parent, a shoulder to cry on, a loan, or a safe place to be. If you continue this mass 'defence' about reaching out for help, all you do is perpetuate agony, and you hold it against yourself that you're not feeling better yet. It's a tragedy that someone who already faces recovery from burnout and breakdown then feels too awful to reach out for help.

If we were to overcome this stigma and this culture of 'grin and bear it,' we would be some way to producing an environment where psychologically injured people get well again more quickly. Sadly, as the culture presides, they have guilt and shame to add on to the initial breakdown as well. My feeling is that this is not insurmountable, and this kind of shift can be made quite quickly even at a cultural and societal level. We have a natural inclination to avoid anything that brings us emotional pain. If we all entered into the spirit of collaboration, we would all be contributing to speeding up everyone's recovery, and so if it happened to us, we'd fear it less, and the spiral would be upwards for everyone.

It might be utopian, but imagine a world where someone is devastated by an accident or bereavement, and everything around them is set up to embrace them whilst they need time to recover. Imagine if we were all to behave in a manner to provide a period of recovery and convalescence from psychological illness or injury; how much better a place this would be! It is this culture of blame with fear and isolation of the psychologically injured that actually perpetuates the suffering. If we need a new pair of shoes, we do something about getting a pair. There is a string of tasks we need to do to rectify this dilemma. If we were to approach psychological injury in the same manner without judgement, with compassion and support, we would provide an environment for revival.

Do you need professional help?

I would say 'not necessarily.' If we did live in an environment of embracing psychologically and emotionally injured people, there might well be less need for professional intervention. However, I do believe that burnout and breakdown and persistent suffering require support. The nature of breakdown is what it says; it's a breakage for the time being, and in its extreme, you will require proper medical and therapeutic guidance. The consequent complexity of the two types of burnout and breakdown, the mixing-up of memories and the re-emergence of emotional injury from previous years can make it impossible to decipher and make progress alone. I do not believe, however, that you are required to sign up for endless years of therapy either.

There are specific features of burnout and breakdown which are aided by being in a relationship with someone else. For instance, someone who feels so wretched after a sexual assault may be helped simply by building a relationship with someone who values them and wants to see them recover and feel better about themselves. In instances of chronic abuse in childhood, people tend to make their mind up that they are not good or likeable people. That is a painful truth about untreated and unhealed trauma: it affects someone's esteem for the rest of their lives, and it dramatically shapes their abilities, choices, and opportunities in life.

I think the most crucial thing for seeking professional support and guidance is expertise and to get someone to hold you in mind or keep you safe while you work through this experience at a deeper level, and at a level that will not only help you recover now, but it will work for you for the rest of your life. It's really important that someone in your life after trauma can keep the vision that you will recover when you can't see it. One of the scariest times after burnout and breakdown is when you literally can see no future at all. You don't recognize yourself, and you don't recognize your life, so therefore, you can't see a future for yourself at all. That's exactly how it is.

So, getting support in place is really about finding someone that believes it's possible to recover and have your life how you want it to be (even with your very real losses based on this experience), the best you can. I think that the support you need is about finding somebody that will help you do a full job now so that you never have to revisit it in the future. If you do a half-job now, it will come and bite you later.

Grasping the journey:

➢ You may as well throw everything you've got at it so that in the short-term it hurts, but you've got a very long-term gain.

➢ You may as well 'wrestle the bear' now rather than have to brawl 'smaller animals' for the rest of your life.

➢ You might as well wrestle shame to the ground rather than have an insidious low-level shame reside within you for a lifetime.

➢ You may as well face your fear of failure now, rather than run the risk of never trying for things you desire for fear of failing.

That is not to say that it will hurt long and hard, but the point of 'wrestling the bear' is about intending to win the 'fight.' The winning in this scenario is reaching a point of wellness, feeling good about yourself with a tenacity that will last you for the rest of your life. The alternative, in my opinion, is that you develop 'scar tissue' to mask the agony. Like all scar tissue, it will protrude and affect other aspects of your life because it's inelastic and, therefore, it will constrain you. It won't move with you and be pliable in the way that you need in order to have a full and successful life.

What framework of support do you need?

The best way to look at this is to treat this like it's a work project, like any other project in life. You see that this has a beginning, a middle, and an end, and you're just going to have to trust me that there's an end, because at this point you probably don't feel there is, but there really is. It's like a story, and it will begin in this harsh and horrific way; it will then have a middle, which is where you're reflecting on what happened and what's happening, and it will have an end where you have recovered, and you have a skillskit for the rest of your life. In terms of the full recovery, I think you have to have support from people without judgement. You already probably judge yourself pretty severely, so you need to seek help from people who know and care about what you now need to regain your strength. You'll have to face that seeking help for the greater good, for the greater good of your family (if you can't feel the desire for yourself just now). If you have family around you, where there isn't judgement and there is support, then that's great. By all means, reach out to them, often friends and family might be the right people. If they are not through no fault of their own, you might need someone outside your inner circle to help guide you through this stormy time. It's possible that relying on friends and family alone runs the risk of prolonged suffering and also re-traumatisation. People close will be significant in your recovery but not necessarily the navigators. There is no hard and fast rule about this, however.

Another part of the structure of support would be being honest with yourself and others about how you feel. Denial doesn't work here. Being authentic to yourself and genuine with your feelings and actions banishes stress. There are many types of psychotherapy, so I would say whatever you feel suits you, but the main criteria would be somebody that you can relate to and get along with. Check what skill base they have, and check they have training and experience in trauma or post-traumatic stress. Preferably, you work with somebody that's qualified to do what we call 'reprocessing work,' where the therapist can support you generally with how you feel, but if need be, they can help you go through specific events to desensitize them. You should be able to reflect on experiences and master them and their control of you.

Key qualities to look for in your professional support

Be able to like them and connect with them.

Appropriate and plenty of experience.

Post-Trauma Work.

Re-processing work.

A core therapeutic qualification.

One of these accreditations: BACP (British Association for Counselling & Psychotherapy). HCPC (Health & Care Professions Council) or UKCP (UK Council for Psychotherapy).

Is this an opportunity?

I believe it is an opportunity, given that this becomes a choice between something that you will fully recover from or something that will be in control of your life and hold you back. I believe it is an opportunity to change this into something that changes your life for the better in some way. Like I was saying before about the energy: the energy that we use to 'squash down' the bad stuff that has happened is energy we can harness to use for valuable things like fun, new desires, new dreams, new ventures. If we are able to release that energy and use it positively, it really is an opportunity to have the life that we want and the ease, contentment, and happiness we deserve.

This is not to say that I do not feel angry and saddened about the atrocious things I see happen to people, but I do believe that by trying to suppress it, we assemble a path of chronic pain. I am continually astonished by the atrocities one human is prepared to do to another, but even more amazed by the courage and extraordinary determination I see in people as they face it. It is this resolve in the face of adversity which consistently heartens me to be part of the solution for those in burnout and breakdown.

Within every burnout and breakdown, I believe there is an opportunity of self-discovery that is part of an inner resilience and skillskit never thought possible. Even with the most knowledgeable intelligent and successful people prior to a burnout and breakdown, there develops an even more formidable and fascinating individual once they have recovered. I wouldn't wish this experience on anyone, but I am committed and have faith that good must prevail. Recovery, healing, purpose, and soul-deep relief can be achieved.

With thorough treatment, you get to mend this latest agony, and you get to 'pick up' the other stuff that you've tried to shelve or ignore. This natural adaptation of the mind and body to cope with 'hard to heal' pains is clever, but it stops working. Burnout and breakdown only happen when your previous defences and strategies are overwhelmed. You might want to honour those pains now so that you can let them go at last and move on with renewed energy. Treatment with guidance helps you release the energy behind all those things that are precariously shelved or squashed right beneath the everyday workings of your mind, body, and soul.

Chapter summary

This chapter is about coming to terms with the fact that you can't do this on your own.

There's no weakness in that, and no judgement about that.

The most compassionate thing you can do for yourself is reach out for help.

There's not a single person in life who's ever lived who hasn't needed a helping hand.

If your symptoms have persisted beyond a month, they're unlikely to go away on their own.

Proper support can guide you so that this becomes something that is the making of you and not the destruction of you.

With the right support, you can reflect on what's happened without becoming re-traumatised.

You can learn about it, understand your symptoms, understand its effects, and understand how you might turn this into something good.

With professional support, you'll likely recover more quickly.

Process 5:
REFLECT & ATTEND – meet and treat yourself with kindness, STRESS HATES that

Why spend time looking at what's happening?

The only reason to reflect on what's happening is for you to feel better fast. I can't see any other reason than for it to aid your recovery and to inform your life from now on. I have purposefully said 'looking at what's happening not what's happened.' This is because everything that is happening now is our best indicator to everything that we need to attend to. The other way of looking at it is that you don't have to dredge everything up from the past, only the things that the present indicates to us are necessary.

So, there is no one-size-fits-all; if it isn't going to aid your recovery and enhance your life, then don't do it. What I'd like to emphasise here is looking at how you think and feel about what's happening rather than only on what's happened.

What's happening now is our greatest guide as to how we can feel better faster. Everything about what's happening now is your clue to your recovery. This may mean looking at connections you have made with past events, or past decisions; it does not mean or necessarily require the recapturing of past experience on a deeper level. People have an extraordinary ability to find patterns in their own and others' behaviour through judgement-free attention, and by identifying these patterns and connections, torment can be laid to rest more quickly.

As I was saying before, in terms of the scrambling-up of the memory, this actually provides you with a capacity to make enormous gains quickly and sometimes by accident.

The most crucial indicator into looking at what's happening is whether your symptoms have persisted; whether you're not feeling like yourself, and you can't function properly. It's an indicator that the only way you're going to get through this is really having a look at the finer detail of what's happening. That doesn't mean looking at every single tiny little painful element of what you've been through. When I was talking about the head picture earlier and I talked about how when you are looking at the 'thread' of memory, sometimes you will unintentionally deal with one thread because it's so similar to another.

Often what's scary about seeking help is the idea that someone will insist on making you do and say things you don't want to. This is completely and utterly counterintuitive in terms of therapeutic support. A practitioner should not insist on this.

On the other hand, I believe that what we don't attend to will be the stuff that's in control in the end, and it will insist we pay attention to it at some point in the future. As previously stated, this is an opportunity; I think if you look at it, you have the very best chance of complete recovery, and simply to say that if you've still got symptoms after two or three months, they're unlikely to go on their own. There is a calming-down time after trauma, i.e. apart from when ensuring someone's immediate safety and pain relief, it is unwise (and inadvisable) if not impossible to embark on any reflection. Reflection and attention, as I say, are for when it becomes clear your functioning is hindered significantly.

This is not the easiest journey by any means. This I believe can be the simplest formula to recovery but an incredibly difficult course. You may have heard it described as a rollercoaster; peeling back the layers of an onion; being on a merry-go-round that you can't get off. It is simple but painful. But as I was saying before, if you 'wrestle the bear' for a short while, you reduce your chances of having to 'wrestle much smaller animals for the rest of your life.'

Discover your emotional modus operandi (E.M.O.)

You will have your own particular way or method of doing something: the way you operate, feel about things and react to things. We all have an E.M.O., and we are all born into one.

An emotional M.O. is looking at what kind of family culture and community you were brought into. Certain feelings would have been acceptable and some not. I call this the template (or the imprint); it's really the pattern of what's emotionally acceptable. Some families will, for instance, have an E.M.O. where there is no anger or confrontation, or no laughter, or no grief.

It's really important to try to discover what your emotional template is. That's because it is the single most powerful thing that stops you from recovering fully; when you have an E.M.O. which doesn't allow you to have your full range of feelings, it creates suffering. When your full range of feelings is not available to you, you have the hardest journey of recovery. Sometimes the simplest of injunctions within your template can have a far-reaching effect when it comes to your experience of burnout and breakdown.

Example: a family template of 'we don't cry' deems full and fast recovery impossible. I have met people who have not cried for literally years though they have experienced great loss. Sadly, this inability to express grief has led them into a life of depression, constant irritation, and even bitterness. Without the tears, you cannot move through the process of grief. A no-crying M.O. would insist that person will struggle with the tears that they need to cry for what they've been through. There are known health benefits to crying. Apart from the build-up of emotion being expressed, it is also a way of reducing stress chemicals for those that are carried within tears.

The way I see this particular 'no-crying E.M.O.' is to understand that crying is a bodily function just like going for a wee: it just needs doing so you can get on with your next thing. In the same vein, if you don't go for the wee and you hold it until you're bursting, all you can think about is that you need to go for a wee. If you don't cry the tears, your tears and grief will be all-consuming and will cause a mess in the long run.

I use the metaphor of walking around with buckets/pails of water. Let's say you have two buckets of tears to cry in order for you to have the best chance of recovery. Every time you cry, you don't cry those same tears again, and it is a little less for you to carry around. If you don't find time to cry them, you may find you will buckle under the weight of having to carry around the buckets full of tears. It's not because you have to be in agony, it's because holding on keeps you stuck and prevents you recovering. However hard it is for you to face your grief, it saddens me more to think that by not getting through it now, you will hinder yourself for way longer than necessary and at worst assign yourself a sentence of private turmoil.

It's not just the 'difficult-to-feel feelings' that get branded as not acceptable, like anger and grief; it can be all kinds of feelings. Feelings like elation, joy, and pride. Maybe in your family's emotional M.O. it is not okay to allow celebration and pride, and so there are those injunctions to discover too.

You will operate best with the full range of feelings you were born to have. When you truly embrace the full range of feelings, you actually feel less of the more 'difficult-to-feel feelings' because you are not expending energy trying to suppress and ignore them.

The full range of feelings

Now I have mentioned the full range of feelings, I want to share what actually I mean by this.

To be fully human and fully available to one's experience in life, we must access and be open to a full range of feelings. That means feelings that we might label good or bad or we might label positive or negative. If we access and notice and experience the full range of feelings, life can be experienced with more ease and gratitude and positivity. In a climate where we do not veto certain feelings, and we access the full range, the chances are we will have positive experiences more available to us. The greatest and most powerful part of the skillskit for life is the embracing of our humanness and our susceptibility to the full range of feelings.

When we veto certain emotions and do our

damnedest to extricate them from our consciousness, it's not as though they don't exist at all; it's that we turn a blind eye whilst actually the vetoed feelings have more control over us than we'd like. When we are all prepared to be open to experience our feelings, they have less power to disturb us, and what we might describe as positive feelings will have more power to revive us and lighten us.

Authenticity

An incredibly powerful part of the process of reflection and soul swimming is to look at being genuine and authentic with yourself and with others. It can be a pretty tricky process when you are disentangling the threads of your emotional M.O.s – or emotional templates, whatever you like to call them. It is made considerably easier when you allow yourself to tap into your emotional life authentically.

It is shocking how many of us spend hours and days in falsity. That's not to say that we don't all have to do things that we don't want to do at times, but really many happy hours are wasted in falsity.

The reason to discover your authentic self is all about giving yourself positivity on a conscious and subconscious level. Every time you do not act authentically, it's like slamming the door in your own face. You reject yourself at a very deep level. Noticing the times every day that you do things that you don't want to do, and when you are not even authentic about how you feel about it. It's incredibly valuable to consolidate your healing when you ask yourself:

'Do I want to do this?'

'Why am I saying yes?'

'Why am I saying no?'

'Do I need to do this?'

'Do I need to do this but be honest that I don't truly want to?'

Do you notice your decisions and your obligations and notice being okay or not being thoroughly happy about it? Every time you are authentic with how you feel, your true self grows and develops and in turn knows that you can grow some more. This may feel like a clumsy and contrived experience at first, but like lots of things, it is invaluable to start practising acting this way even before you believe it to be correct. You will also allow anti-stress chemicals such as oxytocin, and also endorphins to be released when you act authentically, and it gives regard to your true feelings, your needs, and your wants. It's 'free medicine' when you can think of yourself with value. Authenticity with all of your vulnerabilities is your 'self-care card' which you can play with increasing confidence as you recover and heal more and more.

Every time you speak from an authentic place, you nurture a little bit within yourself, even the bits that are hidden away. You come to realise that the world doesn't come tumbling down because you give a true answer. My belief is that when you act with genuineness and authenticity, your subconscious grasps it and allows your self-regard to develop some more. I think about this energetically: whilst you spend time in the falsity as with suppressed emotion, you basically make way for negativity to reside within you, which doesn't allow room for positivity. Part of the reflection and attention to your burnout and breakdown is reflecting on your ability to be real. When you find the courage to make moves towards being authentic to yourself first, and in turn others, you can see your energy shift. Like I said previously, we all have a limit; if you fill your space with negativity in the shape of suppressed emotion, you have used up the space to allow more positive and rewarding emotions and events in. However complex this exchange of energy may appear, the task is really rather simple. You can all ask yourself:

'Am I doing what I want to do?'

'Do I actually want to go out this evening?'

'Do I feel I ought or should?'

Try asking yourself how you feel in a moment, noticing your thoughts, feelings, physical comforts, and discomforts. So, putting aside that there's always going to be things that you have to do in life, my guidance is to use one of these simple not necessarily painful occasions to explore your experience of your own authenticity. This is a useful technique during burnout and breakdown recovery. You don't have to plunge yourself into the most painful of your experiences in order to get to know how you think and act. These are fabulously simple and easy-to-retrieve little 'nuggets' of self-knowledge.

Example: I have worked with people who have faced challenging meetings for years, meetings where they decide on the company vision or look at financial concerns. They find out after years of doing this that they secretly detest it but have done it all the same. Working at being authentic with their feelings, they then went on to find ways to manage this discomfort and to 'use' the energy elsewhere. They found ways to cope with the discomfort or preferably the discomfort doesn't remain because of the awareness. Suspending judgement and embracing authenticity will equip you with a skillskit that will be long-lasting. All pretence is wasted energy.

Due care and attention

It is, in fact, okay even to ask yourself why you made all of your decisions that led to this day. As long as it's without cruel judgement, blame, and shame, it just becomes information for you. This essentially becomes a major part of your recovery, and it supports you if you've been ripped out of your life for days, months, and even years. The experience of burnout and breakdown will prompt self-evaluation of past, current, and future behaviours and decisions. It gives you the opportunity, however unwelcome it was initially, to review, take stock and 're-stock' yourself and your life with what you need and want.

You can reflect fiercely on how your time and energy have been spent. Once you are through the stage of wanting to catch up on time lost, you'll find it tips over to be an appreciation of yourself, your time, and your energy. A knowingness and intelligence of yourself which exudes peace and a certainty that perhaps you've never felt before.

This can throw up all kinds of 'sticky' situations for you personally and professionally, if you suddenly feel you have people around you that are not good for you. Your renewed personal power shines a light on where your energy and time is used in places you don't want to use them. Obviously, this is particularly difficult if it transpires to be a family member or a workplace, but with renewed personal power and authenticity, you get to choose who is in and who is out of your inner circle.

A great tool in this process is to literally draw out your life circle. Get a piece of paper, draw a circle, putting a dot or a picture of a little person in the middle of the circle. This represents you; now you get to decide who and what is in your circle and who and what is not. You also get to decide those things that have to be in there, and you get to decide how you feel about them. You have the pen now (having been completely and utterly out of control), and with your renewed personal power, you get to decide using your circle. A simple little exercise can be fascinating and useful; a chance to sketch out who, and what you want inside and outside of your circle of life.

'Put yourself in the centre of your life and gently challenge yourself to realise you get to invite who and what you want in your life'

This can be one of the changes other people notice when you have been through life-changing events.' Hasn't he changed since the accident?' 'She's never been the same since.'

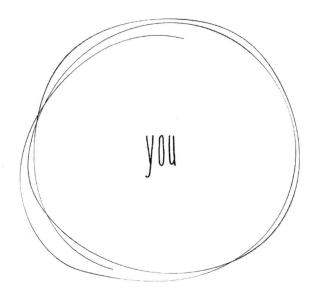

Due care and attention are crucial to recovery and good mental health from now on. Basically, what I mean by attention is to give your experience its due energy. Honour it, and honour you. This comes back to the main premise of this book and its purpose. Giving due attention is the best way of getting through agony the quickest.

'This is the opposite of "carrying on regardless." This is carrying on with due regard.'

My belief is that if you don't give attention to your 'feeling experience,' you are more likely to stay broken down and become broken down again. If you can have your feelings without judgement, you get through them quickly. When feelings are overlaid with judgement, shame, and suppression, they simply last longer or grow within you when you turn a blind eye. They tend to last in a way that ordinary feelings don't. Feelings tend to wash over you as do everyday thoughts; in trauma and breakdown, however, they tend to get larger and in your way if they require some looking after. My indication of feelings that need 'some looking after' is whether they come up again and again. All you need to know is that they are here again, and if they're causing you some distress, then let's shine a light on them for a bit to see what you can do to shift them.

Some related feelings get stuck, and they will persist until they are attended to. Sometimes they might need feeling in order to be moved through; sometimes they just need a little bit of a nudge and a reframing. Reframing is where you take an issue, a thought, and you 'take it outside of yourself' so that you can 'have a word with it' and view it more objectively.

Here is an example of reframing: A client was utterly convinced that they were a 'born loser.' Everything they tried their 'hand at was inept and shit' (in fact the reality was they were successful at almost everything they tried in life, but it didn't feel that way). Together, we looked at the deep belief that he was 'born a loser.' That statement can't actually be true. We are born with many things, but we are not born with a belief about ourselves, that is something that is cultivated over time. When he realised it couldn't be true, he could observe that he had started to believe this as a way to avoid disappointment or failure. This belief of 'I'm a born loser' also, however, meant he couldn't acknowledge and celebrate his successes either, and so almost by default, , the only thing that was illuminated for him was his lack of success and his mistakes. They were the bits that 'fitted' his belief so perfectly and so a cycle of endorsing the belief continued. The reframing process was to see that the belief of being born a loser was like an insurance policy against disappointment and failure. Once it had been reframed and made sense of and made 'friends' with, he could see that it had made sense once upon a time, but now didn't work for him anymore. He went on to be able to see, acknowledge and celebrate his successes. He went on to be as successful but with comfort and ease.

A common example of this for people in professional life is when they berate themselves for not seeking help earlier or not being able to get themselves better, or not being able to avoid the burnout and breakdown in the first place. This is an interesting issue if you take it outside yourself and look at it. Everything in the complexion of your burnout and breakdown makes sense when you look at it; you have done exactly what you could do to manage it. If you reframe the belief that you haven't done well and actually allow an alternative view, and you allow the acknowledgement that you did everything you could with your resources at the time, it begins to 'sit' within you in a completely different way. It sits within you in a much more comfortable way. So that you can move through the 'sticky issues' and be released from the distress they cause.

I want to reiterate once again that I insist that this careful consideration of the finer detail of burnout, breakdown, and overwhelming stress is only necessary when the person is already in burnout and breakdown and/or is unable to function at her day-to-day level. I'm reiterating this to illuminate the issue regarding re-traumatisation. I also want to remind you that the process of recovery is very much focused around careful consideration for each individual person that cannot be set by anyone else at all. So, though all of this is in one book, I want to stress that the 'dance of trauma' will have a different pace and different characteristics for each distinctive individual.

Also, to reiterate, they are not necessarily linear steps; the 'dance of trauma' requires us to accept that the dance is a selection of processes and are not straightforward steps. The 'music' playing can change so whilst actually reflecting on something that may become painful, we might need to change the dance steps and go back and re-establish some safety feelings in order to feel calm and looked after again. Whilst the music keeps changing without your prior knowledge, it can be exhausting; this might be your least favourite dance for a while.

The full range of feelings means you might need to get in 'the swamp.'

In life, you pass good and bad things; you have good and bad things happen. Some things make a change in you; some things don't. Some things are sticky and stick within you but don't change you for the good.

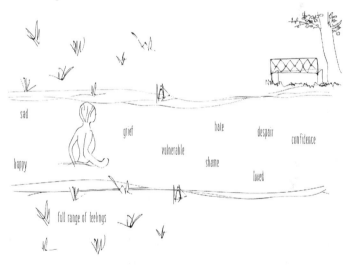

sad

grief

hate

despair

confidence

vulnerable

happy

shame

loved

full range of feelings

Above is an image of the 'swamp.' The 'swamp' exists more and more strongly if you try to avoid it. After you have been shunted out of life and are injured physically and emotionally, you may have to 'enter' the swamp for the first time.

'The swamp' is my way of describing the full range of feelings that's kind of in the way of the recovery that you are looking for. What you need for full functioning and a fully enriching life is in the swamp. You can draw this picture on a piece of paper of a big circle, like a pond or swamp, and on the far side is the sunshine, the 'happy' place, all of the dreams that you're looking for, and on the other side is you now. What's in the swamp is grief, sadness, happiness, anger, all the different and full range of feelings, and it isn't until you can embrace the full range of feelings that you can have what's on the far side of the swamp. You might be thinking, 'I don't want to go in there.' It's new to you; it's new to be able to have a full range of feelings without judgement. I don't suggest you immerse yourself in all these feelings at once; you do not want to overwhelm yourself.

Example: If the full gamut of feelings feels too much, and is not available to you, I might say, 'Okay, you can go over the swamp in a boat, but you need to be prepared to dip your toes in, so that you can start being able to experience feelings with no judgement, so you can learn to allow them.' If you learn to allow them without judgement and fear, you can live creatively, enriched and fulfilled in a comfortable life.

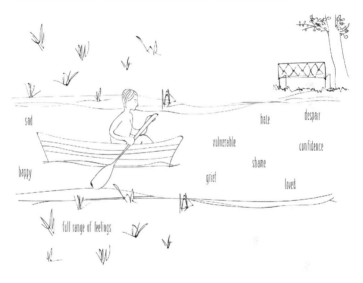

As before, the swamp has all different types of feelings in it. You want to get to the other side where you're feeling well and have the life that you want. It's quicker if you embrace the

full range of feelings. If you'd rather not immerse yourself in the swampy waters, by all means 'take a boat' and be prepared to dip your toes in so that you still have the full range of feelings available to yourself.

Just to restate, we are not trying to create a utopian recovery. We're not looking for 'I never have to think about this terrible thing again.' We're not looking for a decision to be made that only allows happiness; that would recreate more inner pain. What we're looking for is for the experience of the burnout and breakdown to be honoured, learned from and to go in the memory only. To look for a very narrow track of recovery would really be suppressing. We're not looking for perfection; we're looking for you being at ease with being human. It's only in that place, being totally at ease with your humanness that you will be able to have a robust and long-lasting recovery.

You're looking at being able to embrace your full range of feelings, which doesn't mean to say you won't have your favourite feelings, but it means accepting all feelings. By doing this, they wash over you and don't stick to you like toffee. FEELINGS move around you and over you and through you; they are not made to stick. They have only become stuck because you have applied something sticky to them, in order to be able to tolerate them, make sense of them, and reduce their power over you.

Is there a magical secret of robust recovery?

Of course there is no magical secret, unfortunately, but if there were one, I think it would be a magic formula which starts with what I said a couple of chapters ago. Feeling sorry for what's happened to you and talking in a compassionate and companionable way to yourself so that you feel sorry for what you've been through is the beginning of the successful formula.

Secondly, understanding that you're now safe and that you have an ability to understand that you're safe, and you can calm your own system down, as covered in the chapter on Safety.

The 'trauma concertina' or 'trauma bungee'

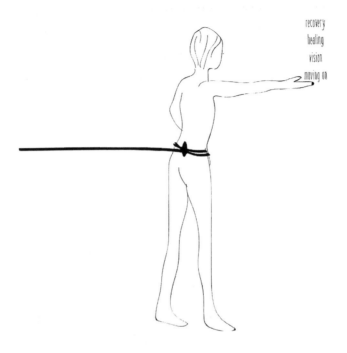

recovery
healing
vision
moving on

The 'concertina of trauma' or the 'trauma bungee' is the unfortunate experience for when you have had the catastrophic thing happen, and it has unearthed or re-awakened things that have happened to you in the past.

The brain, particularly the memory, has a continuum of experience, so anything that's in any way similar, feels, looks, or smells similar to the recent experience, springs like a concertina, everything from birth upwards, basically. That's an unfortunate truth about being in this place – that you're suddenly in a position of not just recovering from the recent event, but your brain is actually throwing up there's something else to recover from too. This isn't the case for everybody; some memories will just wash over you because they are similar, and they don't have any 'emotional charge' about them. For others, however, this will be crucial to your understanding of the particular characteristics of your breakdown experience.

Example: A manager who has burned out recently may find that they did not ever feel good enough for their job. In fact, they have never felt worthy all their life. This culminated into a pattern of behaviour, where they would work many hours, not eat well, not sleep well and continually push themselves to their limits and beyond. In other words, a pattern of behaviour which is trying to make up for something they feel is lacking. If this person can transform that feeling of lacking and learn their emotional M.O. , they will find that they are not lacking at all. In fact, they will find that that is a belief and not a truth. This then frees them up to explore a new belief system, arguably a healthier one and create and maintain a healthier and compassionate relationship with themselves.

Facing the old experiences

It's very difficult for you to face your experiences that predate this one. It can be tough to swallow when you think that very deep experiences thought left behind are now resurfacing again. It can feel as though it's just happened as well. Part of the 'project' becomes even more difficult, even more overwhelming because there's other stuff that's not been attended to and now it's demanding your attention. It's not uncommon. Old stuff may need revisiting for a short while, so you can move on unencumbered. This is not the same as trying to recover repressed memories (memories that are deeply tucked away by the brain). This is about attending to the stuff that is being experienced anew from the past. It is important to understand that this is not something that you invite, it just happens because that's how memory works.

It might be a previous experience of grief that

comes up again. You may find that although your recent experience of an accident appears to have nothing to do with the loss of a loved one, it leaves you finding yourself thinking about them constantly. So, it may be that the recent accident has caused loss and grief, perhaps the physical injury, loss of physical ability, perhaps the loss of a job. And on this continuum you have automatically, so to speak, been drawn back to all your other significant experiences of loss too.

These are the natural workings of the brain. Sometimes it is enough for you to simply acknowledge the link. For some, it may be that you are grieving the loss of your father or mother for the first time. Perhaps it was something that you were unable to deal with fully at the time. You might find this can be consistently overwhelming as other issues come forward to be attended to. However tough this is, and seemingly so unfair on top of what you're already going through, this can be done in the spirit of opportunity and support and does not have to lead to despair. Despair tends to come when you are afraid of the overwhelming feelings and you are afraid of 'going backwards.' It helps for you to remember that this is a normal part of recovery; it isn't unusual even though it can be a tough one to swallow. If you feel afraid of approaching a subject that you felt you had already laid to rest, it is crucial that you feel able to be in control of how you approach that subject now. If you have tremendous fear to begin with but you have a hunch this is necessary for your recovery, you will find time to feel the feelings and move through them. No feelings last, no matter how hard they are to face.

For robust recovery, try to embrace this as an opportunity. A chance once and for all to honour what you have been through, attend to those things, and allow them to go. You'll find they have been taking energy from you this whole time, just to keep them silent and deep down.

It can feel like being on a bungee run (as image below), where you have a bungee rope around your waist, and you're trying to run as hard as you can towards recovery, but you either stand still or the bungee 'drags' you back to attend to the other stuff in your life not fully attended to yet.

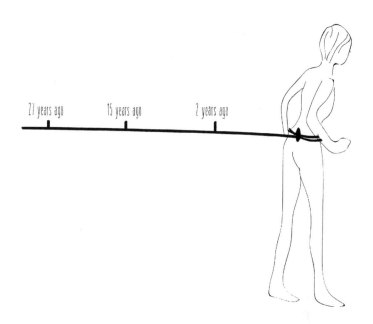

Is there a right or wrong way of reflecting on a trauma?

In my opinion, there is a right way. It's probably easier to say that I feel there's a right way than to say there's a wrong way. The right way, for me, is finding a pace to work at. Rather than going 'hammer and tongs', hurting yourself trying to recover, it's dipping in, looking at what's happening, and then coming out of it and doing something that's not difficult – perhaps watching a film, going for a walk, meeting a friend. The good thing about having professional help, actually, is to have somebody understanding with whom you can look at the difficult experience for an hour, or even 10 minutes and then come away from it for several hours, and then go back to it. The dance sometimes requires us to try not to look at it at all, waiting for a time when you can best tolerate it so that it doesn't exacerbate your symptoms.

This 'dance of trauma': if you go at it severely, it's another way of hurting yourself. It is a challenge to look at stuff that hurts, but by just going into it intensively and aggressively, that's going to hurt you all the more and may prolong your recovery. That's what, in the psychotherapy field, people call re-traumatisation; people can unintentionally re-traumatise themselves without help and make things worse, and that's really not the result you are looking for. The point is to, yes, see it as a project; and yes, rise to the challenge of looking at the very difficult bits of your experiences now and over the years; but in a way that is supported and thorough. If you scare the system (your mind and body) too much, you'll just frighten yourself away from it, and you probably won't end up dealing with it; therefore, running the risk of never fully recovering. Working gently and thoroughly is the 'right' way to go about it. The 'dance of your trauma' will be a very different dance to everyone else's. As I've said before, your reaction is unique, can't be wrong, and is valid. You will have your very own trauma template to discover, which can act as a 'map' to your way through to recovery and healing.

What is the trauma template?

The trauma template is a little bit like the emotional M.O.s. 'Trauma template' is how I refer to the unique imprint that everyone has coming into a traumatic breakdown. My feeling is that when you are shunted into a burnout and breakdown, you are also re-igniting old memories, 'old unresolved issues', in a way that is new and even where you thought they were laid to rest. The trauma template is everything that has ever been traumatic in your life becoming the foundation to everything that you are now experiencing on top of that. As in the 'trauma concertina,' your experiences are all related to each other, some more strongly than others. The trauma template is a useful way of looking at the fact that you rarely come into recent trauma without some previous experience of other stresses, traumas, or near misses.

Discovering what's happened, what's tricky, what's stuck, what is impinging on your life now allows you to discover the 'whole picture' and I call it the trauma template because of all of the things that have concertinaed up. It might be you've been bullied at work or you've lost your job, or you've had an early loss in your life. Exploring everything you've brought to the present day becomes more and more clear that this recent burnout and breakdown doesn't stand alone. Every other experience of loss, bullying, etc. becomes part of your trauma template. That's what a trauma template is, basically. Every single person has one, and it might have no previous trauma, one trauma in it, two traumas, or it might have multiple traumas. Unresolved traumas in the template tend to re-emerge and become re-ignited even when you are convinced they are over and done with. Unresolved pain within you has an uncanny way of getting you to pay attention to it even when that may mean causing you further distress in order to grab your attention.

This chapter has looked at how everything that's

happened to you is important. It's crucial to an understanding and appreciation, actually, of what you've been through, and it's once you've prepared to enter that project that you have a chance of recovering fully. We looked at emotional M.O.s, which we all have: what emotions are acceptable to you and which aren't. Those who don't accept the full range of feelings, 'the swamp' of feelings, will find it the trickiest to recover. Looking at having no judgements about that and being able to accept being fully human speeds up recovery. We looked at the concertina of trauma, where anything that's similar to what you've just experienced recently can concertina up and hit you as though it happened yesterday. We also looked at recovery being an opportunity to deal with old stuff once and for all, so that it doesn't come and 'bite you' in the future. We also looked at the concept of trauma templates, which is basically when the concertina of trauma happens; it gives you the opportunity to discover what's in your trauma template. That's kind of like an imprint that gives you your blueprint of what to look at next and what to concentrate on. We also looked at right and wrong ways of dealing with this; with compassion and with a pace so that you don't become overwhelmed.

However difficult and scary it might be, you never actually get to the point of being overwhelmed again, if that's possible. If there were a right way to achieve a state of complete healing, it would be to look at what's happened with compassion for yourself, pace, and thoroughness.

Chapter summary

The only reason to pay due attention and reflect on your experience is to feel better fast.

Emotional M.O.s are the emotional parameters we have designed or been given early in life that tell us what's acceptable and what isn't. We then think they are innate characteristics of ourselves.

A full life means having a full range of feelings available to you.

Being authentic brings healing more quickly.

Putting yourself truly in the centre of your life and inviting who and what you want in is nourishing and speeds recovery. By this, you honour your experience and yourself.

Recovery doesn't have to be like wading a gloopy swamp.

The 'trauma bungee' is telling you to notice what needs to be paid attention to.

Process 6:
HEALING – smoothing out the STRESS marks

Healing is possible, and if you don't believe that to be true, commit to finding someone who is prepared to believe it whilst you cannot.

Some people might believe that you cannot heal from trauma fully. Healing is a journey towards the smooth scar tissue. It really is a strange battle with oneself, with everything you've ever known before and everything you now face. Sad, unjust, and cruel as it may be, the reality of the arduous journey to recovery and healing is thrust upon you when you are at your very weakest in life. Unfortunately, healing is never as abrupt as the breakage you experience in burnout and breakdown. It is a set of processes that you must engage in. That is the very nature of catastrophic events and traumatic breakdown.

'I am genuinely astounded at the courage I see people find in the face of this desolation.'

You find yourself shunted into a frenzy of distressing, often terrifying symptoms, and then to embark on a journey of healing is remarkable. This is not one symptom alone, this is not one feeling alone, this is where everything is thrown into the air, and every single function and part of your life is affected.

Being able to live beyond the trauma without it impinging on you for the rest of your life is essential in my mind in order to attain fulfilment. The path of healing is in no way a linear journey; it isn't like taking a set of stairs where you see the same sized step each time and take it to the top. I believe it requires the stages/processes, but by no means does that mean you start at Stage One, gaining knowledge, and step nicely and without event to Stages Five, Six, and Seven. Unfortunately, it doesn't work like that. Anyone that has been through this will recognise this to be true.

It's much more like dancing with someone who doesn't know all the steps to follow. Things can happen along the way to throw you back a bit, throw you back to despair for instance. Throw you back to needing to go back to the self-care and safety stage. 'Some dance,' I hear you say. There is no point pretending otherwise. You cannot force yourself through these processes; it's much more appropriate to imagine it as a dance that you commit to. If something comes along that triggers you into a state of panic, for example, flashback, it is crucial you allow yourself to re-establish your safety and your self-care before you proceed to explore anything else. You may find this incredibly frustrating, but if you proceed with a considerate pace and work with compassion for each issue that arises, you basically reduce the risk of pushing yourself into a distressed state. If you manage recovery with care, you don't run the risk of losing the gains that you have made. Every gain is followed by putting that resource into your skillskit. I like to call it, 'installing it.' To learn about your experience, feel the feelings, learn about yourself and install the knowledge for future reference. You grow with your journey; your knowledge of yourself grows as does your resilience. The more aware of your own resilience and resource, the more in control of your own destiny you are.

Healing to the point where the scar tissue over the event or set of events is smooth and elastic requires you to pay attention to anything that may protrude and cause problems for you in the future. That is not to say that you should force the issue, as this will do the exact opposite of what you are trying to achieve. You cannot force recovery and healing; there is no healing or recovery in a place of force, brutality, or lack of control.

Some things may never be okay

Sometimes your healing journey will have to take account of the fact that you can never make some things okay. Your healing journey will need to work with knowing that an injustice has been served you, and you wrestle with it and put it into place within you. Healing can exist alongside knowing certain things may never be okay by us. In fact, you can wrap your healing all the way round the thing that will never be okay by you. This framing of the experience gives your healing power over the injustice.

Your acceptance is part of your healing, and that does not mean you will ever think it's okay. It really means that you don't spend energy fighting an injustice that has already been done. Whilst you fight, your energy is dissipated and taken away from what will nourish and heal you.

There is a dramatic consequence to not

permitting your healing whilst in parallel knowing that that traumatic experience can never have been okay. For instance, it almost always will never feel okay to lose a child; you expect the natural order of things to be that your children will always be with you. Though there is nothing okay about the loss, people are touched by the outpouring of love and affection that can follow a traumatic bereavement. On the other hand, the fight with the injustice can continue to the point of breeding bitterness and rage, which in turn uses energy and gathers momentum. Whilst this is a completely normal reaction to such significant loss early on, feeling and processing the grief is vital to your recovery and healing. Prolonged anger to keep grief at bay takes your healing energy away from you.

How do we know that we are moving towards healing?

Overcoming injunctions

The injunctions that people have spent many years living with, as I said before, are often a key to discovering the paths for healing. Injunctions are things that help you steer your way through life, bearing in mind the family and circumstances that you have come from. These may serve you very well for some time in your life; you may feel they have not served you well at all. The path to recovery and healing often throws these under close examination, yet another thing that becomes 'touched' by terrifying events. During healing, there is an opportunity to sift out the things that you like and dislike about yourself and your lifestyle. So, what can be agonising in the early stages after burnout and breakdown (a loss for instance of everything that you know), later in the process of recovery, you can slowly but surely see this as an opportunity.

Some key elements to healing

Some of the following might seem very basic, but when you are in complete and utter desolation after burnout and breakdown, it's often the simple day-to-day things that will illuminate your recovery. For instance, one of the things I ask people to do is to practice noticing. By noticing, I really mean noticing feelings and things and self and people without judgement. This is so much harder than it seems, but it's a beautiful technique to help you to get to a place where you can notice how you feel without having any strings attached.

For example:

Today I notice I feel panicky.

Today I feel sad.

I am forcing myself not to cry; I tend to do that a lot.

I feel bad when I am late.

I don't like being on my own, but I've always thought I was okay with this.

I only feel good about myself when I am working long hours.

It really matters to me what people think of me.

I always put other people's comfort before my own.

I don't like hugging people.

I haven't really chosen my friendship group.

I eat things I don't like.

I feel anxious a lot of the time.

I get angry quickly; I think I've been like this most of my life.

The things I thought didn't matter still affect me.

Healing means you can have all this 'noticing'

without the overlay of self-torment. Use the words, 'I will practice noticing how I feel, what I like, what I love, what I hate, what I put up with.'

I want to convey to you that although I recommend 'noticing' it doesn't mean I believe it to be easy or that it should come naturally. In actual fact, it often doesn't. You can test out this theory by sitting in a pavement café watching people go by. If you do this, practicing simply noticing, you will find that judgements pop into your head almost without any control whatsoever. So, in a judgement-free atmosphere for yourself, I ask you just to try to suspend the judgement and just notice. When you can do this for yourself, you certainly will be able to judge others less too.

Inner strength & personal power

Feelings of inner strength are good indicators of healing. Remember you are looking to know that the burnout and breakdown happened but that it's not fully controlling you. You are looking for this new flexible scar tissue. There is an inner strength that when it is thorough you will be experiencing anew. This is what I call personal power. This means feeling at the point that you can face difficult situations and rise to tasks when you were previously unable to manage even the simplest of tasks.

This can be experienced as having a spring in your step and knowing that you can approach each day with a refreshed enthusiasm.

'I have seen people recover from the most extraordinary difficult experiences and go on to rebuild their hearts and minds, bodies, and lives.'

Elastic, flexible scar tissue allows your experience. It will always have happened, but in healing, it is less in control of you. You are looking for the scar tissue to exist over the burnout and breakdown, and if you like to give comfort and reassurance of your recovery and healing. I imagine it as being elastic tissue so that it moves with your everyday life. You can never take away that this has happened to you, but now it's safely stored; it is resolved and healed in order for you to move through to better times.

Physical injury

Burnout and breakdown along with a physical injury and/or disfigurement is a significant part of your healing process too. Healing and living with your physical injury will change your recovery journey.

It is also important to recognise where there has been physical injury (e. g. , scarring, loss or disfigurement of limbs, burn scarring, and muscle damage) that may be lifelong; you can absolutely have a relationship with that. It's impossible to do justice to this completely in this book. Physical injury will require recovery, and lifelong injury will require adaptations that are deep and take time. This means taking account of identity and disability and also in acknowledging and facing the mighty challenge of re-establishing the things you've come to know yourself as.

In terms of the processes you may need to engage with, it's not dissimilar to your emotional and psychological injury, but it's obvious, and it's impossible to ignore. Physical injury causes physical pain, as well as grief and anger. It is difficult to embrace something that causes you pain, especially if that pain is caused by another person.

Example: Some of my clients also have described that initially, the pain takes them away from having to deal with the bodily changes they now face. It's only in recovery from the physical pain and injury that we can then address the changes on an emotional level. I have had people say to me 'I can't believe I didn't start dealing with this before.' My answer to this is that our priority always has to be getting physically well first, and we never have the resources to deal with the emotional impact whilst we have to mobilise to get well.

If you have been injured at the hands of another person, you have to tackle the consistent reminders of the event or past events prompted by your injury, scars, and or disability.

So, as well as emotional scars and psychological scars, you are faced with the challenge of having a healthy relationship with your physical scarring too. You can have an emotional relationship with your physical scars that is healthy and that allows you to move on to have the life that you deserve.

The far-reaching process of loss and grief that physical injury propels you into is an arena that is beyond the reach of this book. It is understandable that this is the case, and as with all the other scarring, and things to overcome, this needs to be honoured and needs attention of its own too.

During the healing process, what we're looking for is that somebody gains strength from their ability to survive tragic circumstances. Of course, initially, this feels nothing like it. To have one's body altered either at the hands of another person, by a freak accident or natural disaster is a parallel process to the emotional and psychological journey of recovery. As I was saying when I spoke about the full range of feelings and dipping your toe into the swamp, the full range of feelings is a substantial part of recovering from the emotional impact of physical injury.

Sometimes I have seen and 'borrowed' (referred to) the fact that the physical injury has healed, and this is a good metaphor that the emotional injury will heal too.

For example: A woman with a gunshot wound was struggling emotionally to find the same healing. I asked her to remember and go back in her mind's eye and remember what the gunshot's scarring initially looked like (Interestingly when the emotional healing has not been reached often the image of the wound is still vivid). I then asked her to draw what the initial wound looked like and then asked her what the wound looked like a week later and draw that, and then a week after that and draw that. This woman was able to see and be encouraged by the physical healing. This can be helpful when there is exhaustion about the emotional healing. We have in front of us the images of how the body has healed itself and how a scar has grown over the wound. This can be a useful metaphor that in time the emotional healing will also come. So the parallel journey in recovering from physical injury works both ways. When someone has been close to death, but physically injured in the attack, the person can come to marvel at the body's ability to come back from the near death experience. People can go on with some emotional gymnastics to accept their physical injury scars and or disability at times with considerable strength and resolve.

There is a different kind of adjustment when somebody has physical injury to integrate into their identity. I have been touched over the years to witness within my own personal and professional life and for those in professional life that have shown incredible courage to overcome physical injury. It is entirely possible for you to adapt to your physical injury as well as your emotional and psychological injury. This is an entirely unique relationship which you explore with your experience and with yourself. Adapting to changes in your body can take time, take courage, take patience, and take new experiences in vulnerability. Specialist support is available to help you build a relationship with yourself and the changes in your body (refer to resource list at the back of the book).

Chapter summary

Healing might mean knowing that some things may never be okay – wrap your healing around that.

Overcoming injunctions – if they don't help you on your healing.

A new personal power is the result of your healing.

Where there is physical injury, it may need special attention and time.

Creating 'flexible scar tissue' around your emotional wounds so you can have new life experiences.

Process 7:
VISION & MOVING ON – integrating your skillskit and dealing with STRESS once and for all

You don't have to work very hard at finding your vision again; it is happening all the time as the storm recedes. It's almost something you need not push. It can't be forced, and it comes quicker if you allow it without force. You are now in a position to allow opportunities to wash over you. You have got to a place where you can have idle thoughts again. The agony is behind you, and although it's always happened, you are now in a place where your mind can wander and become creative again; it's now out of 'survival mode'.

A significant agony for you during burnout and breakdown is you lose the ability to have vision at all. In the early hours and days, you will find that you can barely think about what's going to happen in the next ten minutes or the next half an hour. You certainly will struggle to plan the next day or believe you can even rise to the challenge of facing the next day. That might be have been something which once upon a time was so simple for you like keeping an appointment, opening post, or making a phone call.

Seemingly simple tasks become insurmountable, and at times terrifying – the fragility of your abilities so shattered that a once fully working and capable person can be rendered unable to put a meal together or talk on the phone with a family member or friend.

Vision doesn't come like an epiphany. You will find that the trauma storm fog starts to clear for longer periods, and as you begin to feel your abilities coming back, hopes and vision for your future come back too. Living without the vision for a lot of the recovery process means you're working on the healing with some faith only. There is no concrete assurance that you can see in the early days that tells you this arduous journey is worthwhile.

One of the indicators of the journey of genuine healing becoming apparent is when you can reflect upon an idle thought that is visionary. You will find that during supposedly meaningless tasks you begin to experience flashes of excitement about your future. Almost like the flashbulb memories that I was talking about before, these are like flashes of what's possible and of being content without stress and with renewed energy.

Strange as it might seem when the whole body, mind, and soul is shaken to the floor, there comes with it an opportunity to re-evaluate, re-establish and realign your purpose in life. I know this to be true; I have seen it again and again, the ability to overcome and go further than overcoming in the form of embracing the opportunity to renew and reinvigorate. To transform the atrocities that you have experienced in the world into good and better still into excellence is the very best antidote that there can be; the best all round remedy.

The early flashes of renewed ambition are an exciting time for you in recovery. These are the signs of the building blocks of the ability to be able to dream again. The saddening and frustrating thing about burnout and breakdown is that the turmoil is so intense and out of control initially that dreams are stolen in an instant, and the ability to be able to conjure dreams in your mind's eye is stolen in an instant too, in an unfathomable moment.

How cruel that initially there is no escape from

the torment, not even in a daydream. So the early flashes of vision, however momentary, are incredibly significant. These flashes will extend to become moments and minutes of dreaming, however hard that might be to believe now. Once the early flashes of vision are there, although they might not be consistent, they will grow. You will be able to consciously extend these moments before long. Your ability to reproduce them increases your hope of full recovery. This is specific evidence that the brain is recovering, that the nervous system is recovering, that the heart, body, mind, and soul are recovering. You begin to know that you're on the upward spiral.

The intensity of desolation you've been through on every level that is humanly possible, whilst still being alive. Someone that I was working with recently was reflecting what it would be like to have a vision again and was saying 'How is it possible to be so unwell and still be alive?' Whilst I could completely understand her question, I could hardly answer. I could only marvel at her ability to recover from such devastation on a physical, emotional, and psychological level, and then be able to reflect with such a profound question. I was excited that she had come to the point to ask this and was coming away from just surviving the onslaught of feelings and starting to ponder the experience and its repercussions.

Like I said right at the beginning, it is not that people want to die; it is that they have no idea how to live in the face of this experience.

'My heart sincerely goes out to you. You are hardwired to survive, to gather your resources, and if you haven't got any, you would ordinarily go and find some. Burnout and breakdown take away your ability to even think that through let alone reach out to find resources. This is likely to be the most ill you've ever been, yet you still look for answers and your recovery path. It is knowing this desolation that empowers me to write about such a difficult subject in the determination (rather than hope) to offer a path to recovery'

Beyond the despair and hopelessness

It is significant when vision appears, however fleetingly because it gives you real and genuine experience beyond despair. It gives you something tangible, i.e. the evidence that hopelessness has passed. When I was talking about the 'dance of trauma' earlier, it can often be very wearing for your resources, resilience, and patience, frankly. The stopping and starting, the going back two paces for one forward step can be a journey that would try anyone's patience. This seemingly relentless rollercoaster alone can cause symptoms of anxiety and depression, simply because you are asking yourself at your most vulnerable to find courage every single day to face the forward path. Therefore, your flashes of vision (whether you can plan a holiday or you're able to meet a friend) are small yet encouraging steps.

Example: When working with people in recovery, they find it helpful to be occasionally reminded of these glimpses, but on the whole, they usually remember themselves. People tend to remind me of them, so when they feel depressed and despondent, and they feel their own fragility once again, they will often look at me with tears in their eyes and remind me that however desperate they now feel (once again), they know it won't last and flashes of vision are increasing in consistency and breadth. Those early flashes of vision and ideas will become miniature stories within their mind's eye, and they will gain more and more control over them as time goes by. In other words, they will be able to extend them at will in the future; maybe not now, but certainly not too far away. One would never believe that the ability to idly daydream would be so significant in one's life.

Vision becomes increasingly important as recovery enhances. This is because it can become a measure of your ability to override your brain's activity, i.e. , you can now encourage your brain to pay attention to things that you want to pay attention to rather than being at the mercy of its disarray. So something that comes naturally to most other people, you start to re-master.

Extending your ability to have vision, i.e. plan ahead with excitement and positive anticipation, means your body and mind are receiving feedback that things are on the mend. This is psychologically significant and therefore becomes emotionally comforting.

Example: I have witnessed people say to me and show me scars where they've cut themselves and/or tried to kill themselves, map out in front of me what they want their next few years to look like. These being the very same people who when I first met them would not be able to even 'see' the next day. As they have consistently looked after themselves(and noticed and allowed how they can feel), their new visions, hopes, and desires for their future.

So remember your simplest of visions are something to celebrate; it means you're on the mend.

Chapter summary

Glimpses of renewed vision are signs of recovery.

They last longer and longer.

Eventually, you can purposefully extend the time the vision lasts.

You're getting feedback on every level that you are now beyond the despair and hopelessness and reaching repair.

Whilst you're on the mend, you can puzzle together your future plans.

Conclusion:
Moving on with vision and resilience

Moving on means moving on with knowledge and healing; thoroughly drying yourself off (all the bits from the swamp that are still stuck on you) and creating a life for yourself which is nourishing. You are looking towards a place where even if there is stuff that still is perhaps not fully left in the past, that you have some things that are now behind you, and you have all the skills now to deal with the last few challenges that are still hanging around. You are now fully armed to heal yourself. You might need to remind yourself that these tools are never wasted; they are deeper than under your skin. They are so deep that you never lose them; they go with you for the rest of your life, and that's why I believe nothing takes you off your feet in the same way again. It's not that bad stuff won't happen; it's just that you will have a skillskit and an inner personal power that you know that you can rely on.

Integration of your experience

Part of moving on for all of us is how new experiences, good and bad, fit into our lives as a whole; integrating them, putting 'tags' on them and storing them in a useful way. Coming through burnout, breakdown, and stress to the other side where you do not have symptoms anymore, or you have only some low-level issues means you put it into the 'memory store' labelled:

'Recovered, but it will never be okay that happened.'

or

'Recovered, and I'm glad that happened because it changed my life for the better.'

or

'Recovered, and I never want to talk about it again.'

or

'Recovered, and I want to tell everyone about my story.'

There is no right or wrong way to move on. You can now decide outside of the turmoil where you 'store' and how you integrate it into your life. This is your ultimate choice. You get to acknowledge and accept that your rich tapestry of life is not torn to shreds anymore and that it is repaired and put together stronger than ever.

There is no timeline for moving on; you'll know it when you feel it. This too is for you to decide. You might believe that you will come to the end of a line with it. You might, and you might not. It may be that there will be incremental adjustments to be made for months and years to come. It may be that you will be changed by the experience, and you are always aware of your reaction to stress.

People, in general, tend to give other people a 'window' for getting themselves better and nobody knows this more than the broken-down people themselves. You know, and you can feel when people are tired of your predicament and your turmoil. It is this relationship, this felt atmosphere that makes people go 'underground' and not finish the recovery job thoroughly.

That's such a terrible shame, and I'm hoping that this frank discussion about such a difficult time in your life will help you understand that there is no one right way, and you are entitled to take the time you need to recover. Only you know when you are fully well again.

It may simply be that little extra bit of patience from somebody that gives you the permission to heal thoroughly. If we all had that opportunity to change the course of somebody's suffering to recovery, how privileged would the majority of us feel to be able to be part of that? I've often said over the years even to my children that we have a chance every day when we meet people to make that moment a good one; why on earth would we not take that opportunity? When it's something as significant as this, basically, when it's life or death for some, those extra moments of care and consideration may make all the difference.

So, you might be asking yourself what's the difference between vision and moving on, and I'm asking that question too. And I'm fairly sure that it's about actually acting upon the visions; acting upon the dreams; doing stuff and being okay with yourself. It's the doing and the being at ease. It's the testing out of the 'new you.' It's the actual walking the new path you have just spent considerable time and agony paving for yourself. Actually knowing and feeling and believing that the events that 'took you down' are now in the past. It's getting the feedback on every level that your path is real, and it feels all kinds of different ways that you have not been used to. It is getting used to the new, getting used to the unknown in order to make it the known path and to be able to rely on it.

So, moving on is the phase, if you like, of going beyond formulation; it's acting upon the new formulations that you've made for yourself for the way you want to be; the way you want to feel, and the things you want in life. Moving on is acting at a different level where there are opportunities; you can make opportunities now and cease opportunities now.

Moving on is moving forward with your new skillskit.

People at the phase where they can feel the recovery more thoroughly will often describe all of their senses being alive in a different way; particularly people feel that they see things differently, especially colours. The stripping away of everything that was ever known to them and the rebuilding, so to speak, of their emotional, psychological, and physical toolkit, can often mean that everything gradually becomes more into focus. A little like turning a camera lens into focus. When you begin to take the threads of life one at a time, these can be experienced with vividness and renewed satisfaction.

So, moving on is where you truly begin to be able to take bits of control and have choices about what you want to do next with your life. You have your new skills kit, and you have your old skills kit too (because none of that was lost forever; it was simply lost to you during the breakdown). You may find yourself fascinated that all of your skills and experience you acquired before (unless there is brain injury or physical injury that is not recoverable from) the burnout and breakdown are still intact. Moving on is being able to make choices and whilst doing so being able to reflect on what has happened without devastation.

Moving on needs to have an element of being able to look back and reflect what you've been through. Truly moving on, i.e. , leaving something in the past as we would say on a day-to-day basis, means being able to move on and know deep down that you are changed but not broken. That you are moving on with your dreams, with your desires, with your natural fears and trepidation in the knowledge that your soul-deep turmoil found within your burnout and breakdown is over.

Being able to move on in that knowing way, where you are completely assured that your previously overwhelming stress is thoroughly laid to rest.

It's not uncommon for people to try to race ahead with moving on. For instance, people may become tired or disillusioned or just plain bored of the cycle of working through their burnout and breakdown, and so they purposely try to catapult themselves to the end. When this is done too quickly, you can find yourself back in some kind of distress. It doesn't mean that you have gone all the way back to the beginning; it just means that there's something still to attend to, and once it's attended to you can let go of it into the memory banks and then it's time to move on. The ability to look back and feel sorry for what you've been through but have no distress attached to it is an indicator that you're in the process of moving on.

Life choices

Choosing the way you want to live your life after this level of stress is the testament to your recovery and your courage. To have choices is a freedom that you have earned and got back to. You will experience renewed choices aided by your new skills and knowledge that is in your skillskit.

Let's take a look at what's in your skillskit!

You have learned a great deal about yourself.

You know that you have strength of spirit.

You are an expert in what burnout and breakdown are all about.

You know that sometimes behaviours are protecting us from pain or danger.

You know what the full range of feelings is.

You know that you can't get feelings wrong.

You know that you might have a preference about feelings.

You know a lot of things that help you look after yourself.

You know the kinds of friends you would like around you.

You know the kinds of things that you'd like in your life.

You know that feelings experienced move through you and allow you to move on.

You know that the memory is a bit like a concertina; new things can sometimes awaken older things.

You know that being harsh on yourself only hurts you more.

You know the difference between noticing and judgement.

You feel personal power that you've never felt before.

You know fretting about the small stuff doesn't work for you anymore.

You have some new dreams.

You've awakened some old dreams.

You know that some things will never be okay, but that you can heal.

You're the expert in your life.

You're the centre of your life, 'the leading lady or the leading man in your own circle.'

You also now know that you need a bigger skillskit box!

This is why I describe the coming through burnout and breakdown as a- gift. I would not wish the experience upon anyone, of course I wouldn't. I do believe, however, that the strength that one can find within the tumbling and sheer agonies of recovery is exceptional and forever.

Choosing how you want to be with yourself; how you want to talk to yourself; how you want to treat yourself and others is part of a new set of choices. To come through thoroughly means not one single thing is unturned. Burnout and breakdown (even under the worst circumstances) give an opportunity to review. It's a renewed opportunity to reflect, understand, and choose your treatment towards yourself. It's a renewed opportunity to form and re-form your desires, your dreams, your purpose.

So, I've included 'life choices' to signify the arriving in your life in a way that you may never have done before. It's more than 'moving on.' It suggests you are moving away from the arduous journey for getting yourself better. 'Life choices' is about finding your purpose. We are surrounded by incredibly courageous people – men, women, and children. People who have pulled them themselves through incredibly difficult circumstances have gone on to make dreams; live dreams; help themselves and help others. What a wonderful way to leave burnout and breakdown behind; by the actual living and having your 'happy hours and days.'

That doesn't mean there won't be tough times ahead, but they won't have to do with this anymore; now there is a 'skills kit.' The dusty old suitcase used before for shame has been washed down, polished, and now is a shiny suitcase full of the different skills that you've discovered and embraced. You now find you can deal with the smallest of irritations and the trickiest of people with insight and tolerance. This is a better outcome than what you could even begin to conjure if you started at the beginning of this book. To believe in and gain knowledge of oneself and one's dreams again, or for the first time after burnout and breakdown is beyond achievement; it's magical.

For every person living in that positive energy, they give something back to the world just by being someone who has gone through such tremendous life-changing and life-enhancing experience. Your being in the world recovered and healed radiates possibility for other broken souls. I'm not suggesting there is anything that you need to do or that you should do; it's just that the fact that you have come this far shows something extraordinary.

You don't have to run a charity or set out to do good deeds every day in order to live with purpose. The best gift you can give to yourself and the world is to live the life you want to live. The turmoil is behind you, and peace and prosperity have never been so close. The energy that radiates from you and your contented soul gives back to the world, without you needing to do anything. The healing touches every single person in your family and friendship circle, and everyone in your colleague and acquaintance circle. It's like you are using random acts of kindness without needing to be conscious of it at all. So, for those of you who believe in karma, what better way to rebalance Mother Earth?

Those that were most injured are those who become the greatest accidental healers.

Chapter summary

Moving on at your own pace.

You get to choose your new and next steps.

Revel in your new 'skill-kit for life.'

Choose the way you want to integrate your experience.

Enjoy your new choices.

From me to you x

I believe that anyone can recover from the overwhelm, even those of us who are the most doubtful. It is like 'wrestling the bear,' but the decision has to be made to continue the wrestling until you win, and win you will! You can have the life that you want and deserve, and you deserve to be released from your suffering as much as the next person.

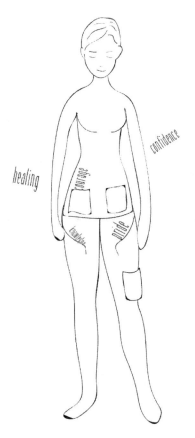

healing

confidence

Recovering from burnout and break-down as you can see is by no means an easy journey; I can't deny that, but it doesn't have to be hell on earth either. There is a lot about the journey from burnout and breakdown to full recovery that is tremendous. To have the opportunity to make friends with yourself; to learn to nourish yourself and to enjoy and nourish others is a gift. You have an opportunity to be the person you want to be through unbelievable suffering and exploration, beyond anything you could have imagined, and you can evolve from the anguish to a personal power that lasts for life.

You come out with the skillskit that's stuffed full; that's bright; interesting, and full of knowledge, but it's not heavy! It's not something you carry; it's all within you.

For those of you who have read this book with loved ones in mind, I thank you on their behalf for your extraordinary dedication and friendship. I hope this has gone some way to providing more than hope, providing possibility and opportunity. They say that what doesn't kill us makes us stronger, but unfortunately, it breaks us first and then needs fixing. Repairing this break is almost impossible to do in isolation. So, thank you to anyone, whether you are a professional, a friend, a loved one, a colleague, thank you for being part of the community that cares.

I hope I have gone some way to helping you understand that the recovery after burnout and breakdown is about engaging in multiple processes. Your relationship with despair will be a major resource for your recovery. When you reach out for help during despair, you will find that act of reaching out will help dissipate the despair more quickly. When you have mastered this, it will become part of your skillskit immediately, and something that you can rely on. This will be by your side during your recovery and always.

I hope that I've made it clear that how you feel and how you've reacted to the traumatic event or set of events can't be wrong. The crucial element of recovery is to understand without judgement what is happening now, much more importantly than what happened then. You can make great gains almost by accident when you build a kindly and companionable relationship with yourself now and forever.

In recovery, you get to move forward with your life, and you get to dream again and have your dreams. The bad stuff will always have happened, but now it is safely stored and is not in charge of you or your life. It has made you an incredible ambassador for revival. You now know that recovery is achievable and preferable even to what went before. Recovery is all about moving forward to better times; better things; better businesses; better work; better play; better relationships. Thorough recovery cannot be anything else. It can only be for the better and the enrichment of the whole.

As your unique spirit is healed and re-enters the world with everything that you are, you can experience truly arriving and getting another turn at being in the world.

INFORMATION ON SERVICES and ANNA's WORK

If you've enjoyed this book, please do give a 5 star rating on Amazon and help this important message reach many more people!

FOR FREE PRODUCTS and information on courses and working directly with Anna go to www.annapinkerton.com

TRAINING: 'Anna Pinkerton's Kindness Incorporated Training Academy' (For courses & booking in-house training with Anna)

'Smile Again' Approach for personal growth and professional training

Book through www.annapinkerton.com

SPEAKING ENGAGEMENTS & WORKSHOP BOOKING

For enquiry & booking form via www.annapinkerton.com

ANNA PINKERTON

Want to work directly with Anna?

Anna offers a highly discrete service.

Via www.annapinkerton.com

Email anna@annapinkerton.com

RESOURCES

Useful words to search on web:

Art Therapy

Breakdown

Breakthrough

Burnout

Compassion based treatment

EMDR

Meditation (and meditation Apps)

Mindfulness

Positive psychology

PTSD

Resilience

TIR

Trauma recovery

Vicarious traumatisation

Another Way Associates – For recovery & healing at an organisational & institutional level

'Having another way is good'

Business Manager: Ettie Brisk 07889 834706

ettie@anotherwayassociates.com

http://www.anotherwayassociates.com

Berkshire Traumatic Stress Service

25 Erleigh Rd
Reading
Berkshire
RG1 5LR

0118 9296 439

http://www.rbwm.gov.uk/

British Association for Counselling and Psychotherapy (BACP): For qualified practitioners

BACP House
15 St John's Business Park

Lutterworth

LE17 4HB

01455 883300

http://www.bacp.co.uk/

Changing Faces – for support with lifelong disfigurement

The Squire Centre

33-37 University Street

London

WC1E 6JN

info@changingfaces.org.uk

www.changingfaces.org.uk

Changes Faces - emotional support and advice call 0300 012 0275

support@changingfaces.org.uk

Drug and alcohol dependency support

Addaction

67-69 Cowcross Street
London
EC1M 6PU

020 7251 5860

http://www.addaction.org.uk/

Adfam – Support for families affected by dependency

25 Corsham Street
London
N1 6DR

http://www.adfam.org.uk/

Adsolutions

135-141 Oldham Street
Manchester
M4 1LN

0161 8312400

http://www.adsolutions.org.uk/

Mind

15-19 Broadway

Stratford

London

E15 4BQ

020 85192122

http://www.mind.org.uk/

Turning Point – London Office

Standon House

21 Mansell Street

London

E1 8AA

Turning Point – Manchester Office

The Exchange

3 New York Street

Manchester

M1 4HN

http://www.turning-point.co.uk/

EMDR Association UK and Ireland: For re-processing and consolidation work

(Eye Movement Desensitisation and Reprocessing Therapy)

EMDR Association UK and Ireland
PO Box 3356
Swindon
SN2 9EE

www.emdrassociation.org.uk

Food Addiction Support

ACORN Food Dependency Recovery Services

PO Box 50126
Sarasota
FL 34232-0301

941-378-2122

http://foodaddiction.com/

Food Addicts Anonymous

529 NW Prima Vista BLVD
#301A

Port St. Lucie
FL 34983

772-878-9657

http://www.foodaddictsanonymous.org/

National Centre for Eating Disorders

54 New Road
Esher
Surrey
KT10 9NUUK

+44 (0)845 838 2040

http://eating-disorders.org.uk/

Health & Care Professions Council (HCPC) – For accredited therapists & health care professionals

Park House
184 Kennington Park Road
London
SE11 4BU

0845 300 6184

http://www.hcpc-uk.org.uk/

CATTI Protocol
Art therapy Institute of the Redwoods

Director: Linda Chapman

10151 East Road
Redwood Valley
CA 95470

001-707-485-0105

info11@arttherapyredwoods.com

Peter Orlandi-Fantini

Psychotherapist, Teacher, Supervisor

Sherwood Psychotherapy Institute
Nottingham, England

07736 617100

peterof@spti.net.com

peterof@btinternet.com

PTSD Support

Dr Lori Beth Bisbey, CPsychol, AFBPsS, CTS, DipFMSA, MEWI, WPCC

Consultant Psychologist, Whole Person Certified Coach

Owner Bisbey Ltd and Wolf's Fire Ltd

Author of Counselling for PTSD: Traumatic Incident Reduction and Related Techniques (Wiley and Sons, 1998)

www.bisbeyltd.com

www.wolfsfire.com

First Light Trust – Supporting forces veterans

Charmy Rise
Barker's Hill
Semley
Shaftesbury
SP7 9BH

0845 519 9401

First Light – Yorkshire Office

FirstLight Trust
63 Newborough
Scarborough
YO11 1ET

0845 519 9402

http://www.firstlighttrust.co.uk/

SSAFA – Support for members, veterans and families of the forces

SSAFA Central Office
4 St Dunstans Hill
London
EC3R 8AD

0845 2417141

www.ssafa.org.uk

Refuge: For those experiencing domestic abuse

4th Floor
International House
1 St Katharine's Way

London
E1W 1UN

0808 2000247

http://www.refuge.org.uk/

The Centre for Trauma, Resilience and Growth: For trauma survivors & trainings

St Anns House
114 Thorneywood Mount
Nottingham
NG3 2PZ

0115 8440586

http://www.nottinghamshirehealthcare.nhs.uk/
our-services/local-services/specialist-
services/prescribed-services/trauma/

Trauma Center at Justice Resource Institute: World leading experts and researchers into PTSD.

1269 Beacon Street
Brookline
MA 02446

617-232-1303

http://www.traumacenter.org/

Traumatic Incident Reduction Association (TIRA): For trauma re-processing work

TIRA
5145 Pontiac Trail
Ann Arbor
MI 48105

Toll Free: 800-499-2751 (in the USA, Puerto Rico, Virgin Islands, and Canada)
Phone: 734-761-6268

www.tir.org

UK Council for Psychotherapy (UKCP): Finding a qualified therapist

2nd Floor
Edward House
2 Wakley Street
London
EC1V 7LT

020 7014 9955

http://www.ukcp.org.uk/

UK Psychological Trauma Society (UKPTS)

http://www.ukpts.co.uk/site/trauma-services

Victim Support UK

0845 30 30 900

https://www.victimsupport.org.uk/

**Women's Aid: For those
experiencing domestic abuse**

PO Box 3245
Bristol
BS2 2EH

0808 2000247

http://www.womensaid.org.uk/

Reading list

Andrews B., Brewin C. R., Rose S. & Kirk, M. (2000) **'Predicting PTSD symptoms in victims of violent crime: the role of shame, anger, and childhood abuse'** Journal of Abnormal Psychology

Arguile R. (1992) **'Art therapy with children and adolescents'** in 'Art therapy, a handbook' edited by Waller D. & Gilroy A. Open University Press

Betenksy M. G. (1995) **'What do you see? Phenomenology of therapeutic art expression'** Jessica Kingsley Publishers (JKP)

Bisbey S. & Bisbey L. B. (1998) **'Brief therapy for post-traumatic stress disorder, Traumatic Incident Reduction and Related Techniques'** Wiley

Bledin K. (1994) **'Post traumatic stress disorder once removed: a case report'** British Journal of Medical Psychology Vol 67, Pg. 125-9

Brown Brene. (2013)'**Daring greatly, How the courage to Be Vulnerable Transforms the Way We Live, Love, Parent and Lead'** Penguin

Chapman L. (2014) '**Neuro-biologically Informed Trauma Therapy with children and adolescents: Understanding mechanisms of change'** Norton

Davidson L. & Baum A. (1994) '**Psycho physiological aspects of chronic stress following disaster'** in '**Trauma and disaster'** Cambridge University Press

Dyregrov A., Gupta L. & Gjestad R (2000) '**Trauma exposure and psychological reactions to genocide among Rwandan children'** Journal of Traumatic Stress Vol. 13

Eth S. & Pynoo's R. (1985) '**Post traumatic stress disorder in children'** American Psychiatric Press

Eth S. & Pynoo's R. (1994) '**Children who witness the homicide of a parent'** Journal of Psychiatry, Vol 57 pg 287-304

Furnam E. (1986) **'When is the death of a parent traumatic?'** The Psychoanalytical Study of the Child Vol. 41 Pg 191 207

Gelder et al (1994) **'Classification of reactions to stressful experiences'** in Concise Oxford Textbook of Psychiatry, Oxford University Press

Gil E. (1991) **'The healing power of play, working with abused children'** The Guilford Press

Heineman T. V. (1998) **'The abused child, Psychodynamic understanding and treatment'** The Guilford Press

Herman J. L. (1992) **'Trauma and recovery, from domestic violence to political terror'** HarperCollins Publishers

Kennedy H. (1986) **'Trauma in childhood'** Psychoanalytical Study of the Child Vol 41 Pg. 209

Kinchin D. (1994) **'Post traumatic stress disorder'** HarperCollins Publishers

Van der Kolk, McFarlane & Weisaeth (1996) **'Traumatic stress, the effects of overwhelming** experience on mind, body and society' The Guilford Press

Laor. N., Wolmer. L., Reiss. A. & Muller. U. (1998) 'The function of image control in the psychophysiology of post traumatic stress disorder' Journal of Traumatic Stress

McCann L. 7 Pearlman L A. (1990) 'Vicarious traumatisation: A framework for understanding the psychological effects of working with victims' Journal of Traumatic Stress Vol. 3, No.1 Pg 131-149

McCaughey, Hoffman, & Llewellyn (1994) 'The human experience of earthquakes' in 'Trauma and disaster' Cambridge University Press

McColl M. A., Bickenbach. J. & Johnston. J. (2000) 'Changes in spiritual beliefs after traumatic disability' Arch, Phys Med Rehabilitation, Vol. 6, Pg. 817-23

McColl M. A. & Bickenbach. J. (2000) 'Spiritual issues associated with traumatic-onset disability' Disability and Rehabilitation Vol. 22

Mullarky K. & Pfeffer C. (1992) **'Psychiatric treatment of a child suicide survivor'** <u>Crisis</u>, 13/2 Pg 70-5

Regel S. & Joseph S. (2010) **'Post Traumatic Stress, The Facts'** Open University Press

Schavarien J. (1992) **'The revealing image, analytical art psychotherapy in theory and practice'** Routledge

Schavarien J. (1999) **'Art within analysis: scapegoat, transference and transformation'** <u>Journal of Analytic Psychology</u> Vol.44 Pg. 479-510

Silva R. R., Alpert M., Munoz D. M. & Singh S. (2000) **'Stress and vulnerability to post traumatic stress disorder in children and adolescents'** <u>American Journal of Psychiatry</u>. Vol. 157 Pg. 1229-35

Terr L. C. (1991) **'Childhood Traumas: An outline and overview'** <u>American Journal of Psychiatry</u> 148:1 pg. 10-19

Udwin O. (1993) **'Annotation: Children's reactions to traumatic events'** <u>Journal of Child Psychology and Psychiatry</u>

Ursano R, McCaughey & Fullerton C. (1994) 'Trauma and Disaster, individual and community responses to the structure of human chaos' Cambridge University Press

Wax Ruby. (2014) 'Sane New World: Taming the mind' Hodder

Weine S. M., Becker D. F., Levy K. N. & Edell W. S. (1997) 'Childhood trauma histories in adolescent inpatients' Journal of Traumatic Stress

Weisaeth L. (1994) 'Psychological aspects of technological disasters' in 'Trauma and disaster' Cambridge University Press

Sims D. W. & Bivians B. A. (1989) 'Urban Trauma: A recurrent disease' Journal of Trauma Vol. 29, No.7 Pg. 940-7

Wright K. & Bartone P. (1994) 'Community responses to disaster: the Gander plane crash' in 'Trauma and disaster' Cambridge University Press

Yule W. & Williams R. (1992) 'The management of trauma following disasters' in 'Child and

Adolescent Therapy, a handbook' edited by
Lane D. & Miller A. Open University Press

About the author

Anna Pinkerton is an art psychotherapist, a therapeutic coach, trauma practitioner, and speaker. She has a first class degree and has dedicated her psychotherapy career to understanding post-traumatic stress. She enhanced her foundation training by studying three re-processing techniques EMDRII (Eye movement desensitization re-processing) TIR (Traumatic Incident Reduction) and CATTI (Chapman Art Therapy Treatment Intervention) protocols. She incorporates these trauma specific methods amongst a generic model of therapeutic coaching. She has been in practice for almost 25 years.

Her training and experience have given her a broad understanding of the effects of traumatic experiences and chronic stress throughout the lifespan.

Having spent all of her working life specialising in post-traumatic stress, in 2011 Anna was physically assaulted and ended up with it.

Anna became determined to transform this experience into a gift and became able to recognise the extraordinary opportunity she had in experiencing post-traumatic stress from the inside. Her knowing the reality of the storm within which you can find yourself within seconds truly astounded her. Anna set out to repair herself emotionally (if not physically) from feeling utterly broken and was able to marvel at the insight she was gaining into recovery. She's knows recovery is achievable. She doesn't just know it to be true – she doesn't just believe it to be true – she's done it.

Anna now fully recovered is director of CHAPTERS, a creative psychotherapy practice offering work with children, teens, families and adults in Derbyshire and the East Midlands. She is the founder of 'The Magic Science of Kindness' a training which creates learning opportunities for individuals and institutions to engage in a philosophy of kindness from the inside out. Anna also speaks about and teaches the 'Smile Again' approach. She's known for her warmth and humour.

Anna herself offers a unique therapy and coaching service to people from all around the world. She specialises in working with business owners and those facing the rigours of professional life. She has ground-breaking ideas on prevention of stress and burnout and has formulated a philosophy of living with ease which will be the subject of her next book.

Everything in this book is what she has discovered in working with hundreds of emotionally, psychologically, and often physically injured people, and of course her own story.

21933406R00181

Printed in Great Britain
by Amazon